THROUGH CHILDREN'S EYES. 1.

Ideas for an integrated approach to Religious Education for younger children.

DISCOVERING THEIR WORLD

GEOFFREY DUNCAN

DENHOLM HOUSE PRESS

Robert Denholm House, Nutfield, Surrey, RH1 4HW

First published 1973

© *1973 Geoffrey W. Duncan*

ISBN 0 85213 072 4

Printed by
Cox and Wyman Ltd.,
London, Reading and Fakenham

CONTENTS

To

JANE AND **RUTH**

with love

GENERAL INTRODUCTION

Religion is a part of life, and within each one of us religious development inter-acts with the various other aspects of the human personality. Because of this, when we are planning the curriculum, we need to consider the religious development of the children in our care, and their relationships in the school.

The contents of this book suggest in a variety of ways how religious education can be integrated into the school curriculum.

Whilst the material suggested in the sections is intended for use in First Schools, and the first year of the Middle Schools, covering the age range 5–9 years, there is also a place for it to be used in the Church situation where Holiday Clubs and similar projects are arranged.

There are four main themes, *Creation*, *Nature*, *All About Me* and *Food*. Each theme is broken down into five or six sections in which one of the basic aspects of the theme is developed.

There are a variety of suggestions within each section for the use of Biblical material, hymns and songs, prayers and source material, all of which can be used to advantage with many other areas of the curriculum. There is also an appendix which supplies a list of useful names and addresses from which source material for the themes can be obtained.

As the age and ability range for which the book is intended is wide it is anticipated that the suggested material will be used as a guide which will be augmented and adapted to suit the individual situations in which it will be used.

The development of each section is based on the theory and practice of an Integrated Curriculum. The Starting Point should be a stimulating occasion for the children. This is not dealt with at length, as the development must depend largely on the facilities available in each school. After the commencement of each section, each of which can stand in its own right, the suggested material should be used

5

according to the needs of the children, and the way in which individual teachers wish to integrate the suggestions. It is anticipated that teachers will feed in their own ideas. In some instances it is desirable to follow on to the next section but where this is not possible material from one section can be used along with that of another section, which may be the way in which some people will wish to work for the *All About Me* theme.

GEOFFREY W. DUNCAN

Poole,
Dorset.
1973

ASSEMBLIES

Whilst there are title suggestions for Assemblies within the framework of each section it is appreciated that some teachers may wish to alter these for titles and captions of their own which can be displayed in the hall. This is good, and when it happens the sections will have been developed in the way best suited to each class of children. The essence of this activity is to ensure, in the majority of the sections to each theme, that the work is brought to a climax in which the children are involved.

Material for the Assemblies will need to be drawn from all that will happen as the sections are developed. The suggested titles are to be used only as guidelines, moving towards the point whereby the children will engage in an Act of Worship which is joyful, bright and meaningful to them.

There will be occasions when parents will be involved and share in the worship. As we build relationships with our children it will be beneficial to create an atmosphere where this happens with the parents too, thus realizing a community, and caring body, of people.

Possible sequences of events for Assemblies in which the teacher as Leader will need to act as co-ordinator are as follows:

A. 1. Opening Music whilst the children assemble.
   2. A poem or verse according to the theme.
   3. A hymn.
   4. Highlight the theme by involving the children in an activity / readings of their own work OR selected frames from a filmstrip / transparencies.
   5. Prayers.
   6. A hymn to be sung as the children depart, and continued as they return to their rooms.

B. 1. Opening Music.
   2. An activity to highlight the theme. This can be done through Drama / Readings or the use of Visual Aids.
   3. Prayers.
   4. Hymn.
   5. Music as the children depart.

C. 1. Music by the children.
   2. Prayers.
   3. Hymn.
   4. Poem.
   5. Quiet Time before departure.

D. 1. Music.
   2. Focus attention on a collage / frieze / any other static visual aid. Involve the children in conversation.
   3. Poem.
   4. Hymn.
   5. Prayers.
   6. Focus attention on (2) above whilst suitable music is played in the background.

E. 1. Assemble quietly with attention being focussed on a display of items made by children. This can be a centrepiece. Involve the children in conversation.
   2. Prayers.
   3. Hymn.
   4. Music as the children depart.

F. 1. Movement activity by a group as the majority of the children assemble.
   2. Hymn.
   3. Prayers.
   4. Poem.
   5. Movement activity by the group whilst the majority of the children sing a suitable song or hymn.
   6. Quiet time before departure.

THEME ONE

CREATION

1. The Seasons

The method for developing this section will depend upon the time of year at which it is started. Relevant items from the world of nature can be used as Starting Points, e.g. an arrangement of spring flowers, June roses, a display of Autumn leaves, a bucket of snow, icicles or bare twigs.

Environmental Visits
These can be made to the park, woodland, or any other suitable place. If it is possible to arrange two visits, one at the beginning, and another towards the end of a term, the children will be able to observe changes which have taken place.

Language Development
The children will readily discuss the relevant season according to their experiences which will be largely influenced by their environment. Some will be able to talk about their gardens, others about life in the town, or country, and some will be able to talk about life by the seaside during the different seasons. What are the children wearing? What is the weather like? Is it hot or cold? Is it windy with plenty of rain, or is it frosty?

SUGGESTIONS FOR WRITTEN WORK: Relevant news stories and reports on visits can be recorded in a Group or Class Work Book. Creative writing can involve the children in seasonal imagination, the content of which can be varied.

STORIES TO BE READ OR TOLD:
The Snowy Day by Ezra Jack Keats (Bodley Head). A film-strip is also available from Weston Woods Studios Ltd.
Henry's Busy Winter by Dora Thatcher (Brockhampton)
Topsy and Tim's Snowy Day by Jean and Gareth Adamson (Blackie)
Spring, Fall and *In Between* by S. P. Russell (Concordia)
Other stories can be selected from *Stories for all Seasons* (National Christian Education Council)

Make up a Year Series: 'Suddenly it's Spring', 'Summer Sun', 'In the Autumn', 'Nip of Winter', all by Peggy Blakeley (A. & C. Black)

POETRY:

Spring Song – poet unknown
Autumn Fires by R. L. Stevenson
One Misty Moisty Morning – poet unknown
} from *Poetry Panorama, Book 1* (Odhams)

Snow towards Evening by Melville Cane from *Poetry Panorama, Book 2* (Odhams)
Stopping by Woods on a snowy evening by Robert Frost from *First Poems* Book 3 (Schofield & Sims)
'*Summer Sun*' by R. L. Stevenson from *A Child's Garden of Verse* (Collins)
Poems by traditional writers such as Lord Tennyson, William Wordsworth, and Walter de la Mare can be found in the Landscapes and Seasons section of *The Swinging Rainbow* – poems for the young selected by Howard Sergeant (Evans)
Red in Autumn by Elizabeth Gould from *Come Follow Me* – poems for the very young (Evans)

Art and Craft

Wall collages or friezes can be made to depict the character of each season. All Things New can be the title of a collage for the period leading up to Easter. The work on Autumn can follow naturally from Harvest activities whereby the shades and happenings of this season blend easily with work which may have already been done. A seaside scene for the Summer and a snow scene for Winter with suitable titles supplied by the children will add to the learning and pleasure to be derived from these seasonal activities.

Science

An Interest Corner or a larger area of the room, can be established for each of the seasons. The children will readily bring all sorts of items for display. The Interest Area can carry the names suggested, relevant to the season:

All Things New (for Spring and Easter)   Autumn Colours
Sunny Summer Days   Winter

The words from Genesis 8: 22 as in the New English Bible can be written on a card and placed in the display. This will highlight God's activity in each season. For the Spring, 'All Things New' will be conveyed through Spring Flowers, new leaves and buds. 'Sunny Summer Days' can be emphasized by displaying items used for holidays, picnics, and outings to the beach. For the Autumn the following verse could be used:

> *Green, yellow, orange, red and brown,*
> *All these colours can be seen*
> *As the leaves come tumbling down.*

The single word Winter will help to suggest the bareness of the season with perhaps a twig and one or two more items on display.

Social Studies

Reference can be made to the climate and seasons of the Holy Land where there is a long dry season from May until October. Mount Hermon has snow on its peak all the year round. In North India there is the season of heavy rains as well as the dry season when there are frequent droughts. In Australia people are able to swim and sunbathe on Christmas Day when they have their Christmas Dinner on the beach. Other comparisons with our seasons can be made. Children in the class may be able to contribute towards a talk about seasons in other lands. Some may have lived abroad, and others will have spent winter or summer holidays in other countries.

Music

The Seasons (Vivaldi), ASD 367
Pastoral Symphony (Beethoven), HMV ASD 2565
Autumn Leaves – A movement song from *Merrily Dance and Sing* by Gwendoline E. Holt (Boosey & Hawkes)

Religious Education

The caring of plants throughout the seasons can be emphasized by planting bulbs in the Autumn, tending them through the Winter, and watching them bloom in the Spring. After the planting use the prayer:

We have enjoyed working the fibre, handling and planting

the bulbs. We look forward now to watching them grow. We have put them ready. We will look after them. You will make them grow. (From *Praying with Juniors* by Jack and Edna Young – National Christian Education Council)

BIBLICAL MATERIAL
While the earth lasts (Genesis 8: 22)
Rain comes at the proper time on the land (Deuteronomy 28: 12)
God made Summer and Winter (Psalm 74: 17)
Snow, frost, ice, the wind – all are mentioned in Psalm 147: 16–18, and Psalm 148: 8

PRAYERS: The children can compose their own variety of prayers, some of which can be used in the classroom, and others at times of Assembly. Prayers for Winter and Summer can be found in *Please God* by Beryl Bye and Joyce Badrocke (Church Pastoral Aid Society). There is also a section entitled 'The Season' in *Time and Again Prayers* compiled by Janet Cookson and Margaret Rogers (O.U.P.)

HYMNS
General
The Seasons (From *Sing a New Song* by Bridget Ball, Religious Education Press)
For the beauty of the earth
Praise be to God for the wind that blows (*New Child Songs*, Denholm House Press)
Springtime
My Garden (From *Sing a New Song* by Bridget Ball)
Praised be our Lord for the turn of the year (From *The Morning Cockerel Hymnbook* – Rupert Hart-Davis)
The whole bright world rejoices now (From *The Morning Cockerel Hymnbook*)

What do we see on a warm Spring day	From *New Child*
Sunshine in the city	*Songs*, Denholm
Seeds and bulbs are all asleep	House Press

Summer
I love the Sun

We wake up with the sun	From *New Child Songs*
Thank You, God, for lovely sea	

Autumn

O lovely world of colour
Autumn leaves are fluttering down } From *New Child Songs*

Winter

Snowflakes
The Lamp } From *Sing a New Song* by Bridget Ball

See how the snowflakes are falling
We thank you, loving Father God } From *New Child Songs*

ASSEMBLIES: Titles and suggestions can be found in the Art and Craft and Science sections. Each season will bring forth plenty of response from the children and this will enable the Assemblies to be bright, refreshing acts of worship.

Further Source Material

FILMSTRIPS

The Seasons (Parts 1 and 2) from the Society of St. Paul
This Wonderful World – selected frames showing late Summer and early Autumn (National Christian Education Council)
We enjoy God's gifts – selected frames showing autumn (N.C.E.C.)
God's Autumn World
God's Care in Winter } These are suitable for the very young children (Concordia Films)
God cares through a dependable world – selected frames showing Spring-time. Suitable for very young children (Concordia Films)
God cares through growing things – selected frames showing Winter (Concordia Films)

TRANSPARENCY

Still life with apples – Cézanne (Tate Gallery Publications)

PRINTS

The Hunters in the snow (Brueghel)
Countryside (De Gallard) } Athena Reproductions Ltd.

WALL PICTURES

Summer and Autumn frieze books (National Christian Education Council)

Sowing Seed ⎫
Winnowing ⎬ from the *Life in Bible Times* set by Wilbur Adam

Helping in the garden – Friends Picture set by Frances Hook
God takes care of the birds ⎫
God takes care of the animals ⎬ the *Present Day picture set* by
God gives me beautiful things ⎬ Frances Hook
God sends the rain ⎭

The above picture sets are available from the National Christian Education Council.

REFERENCE BOOKS

The Seasons series: *Spring, Summer, Autumn and Winter* by Edna Johnson (Basil Blackwell)

A Book for Spring / Summer / Autumn / Winter by Mollie Clarke (Wheaton)

What to look for in Spring / Summer / Autumn / Winter (Ladybird)

Observe and Discover in Autumn, Winter and Spring, Summer by F. Dickinson and I. R. Worsnop (Macmillan)

2. Space

Starting Point

What is space? As adults, teachers could ask themselves, what is our conception of space. Visit the games field, or if this is not possible, the hall, for a P.E. lesson on movement of the body. The children should be asked to think about leaving a space between themselves and their neighbours. Concentrate on the aspect of using the space all around whatever the movements may be.

Language Development

In the course of a talk about the space which they used in their P.E. lesson, lead the children into thinking about the men who travel in space. Talk about TV programmes such as Star Trek and other relevant programmes when this section is being used.

SUGGESTIONS FOR CREATIVE WRITING
A Journey in Space
What I found on Space Station X

STORIES TO BE READ OR TOLD
Adventures in Space – a series of three books in each of four sections (Rupert Hart-Davis)
Peter the Rocket by Helen C. Caddy (Oliver & Boyd)
Dougal and the Space Rocket by Jane Carruth (Odhams)

POETRY
I had a little Space Man by Michael Ivens from *Happy Landings – poems for the youngest* chosen by Howard Sergeant (Evans)
Rocket to the Moon by Douglas Gibson from *The Swinging Rainbow – poems for the young* selected by Howard Sergeant (Evans)

Drama

The children can create their own ideas of a count-down, and lift-off; a journey through space encountering various moving objects such as meteors, and finally landing on an unknown planet where there are strange creatures roaming the surface.

These suggestions will need to be discussed with the children, and they will be able to contribute further ideas, using their imaginations as to what the strange creatures will look like. They can work as individuals, pairs or small groups according to whatever they represent. Sound effects will be necessary; therefore it will help beforehand to listen to the following recordings:

Space Experience – Studio Two No. TWO 393

Listen, Move and Dance No. 4 – Moving Percussion and Electronic Sound Pictures CLP 3531

The Planets Suite (Holst) – B.B.C. Symphony Orchestra SZ 234 (E. J. Arnold)

Rhapsody in Blue (Gershwin) – Opening section, SXL 6411 (Decca)

Sprach Zarathustra – Bronhill SCX 6359

2001 Space Odyssey – 2310073

Art and Craft
Models of rockets, lunar modules and launching pads can be made from scrap materials. Astronauts and 'men in the moon' can be made from liquid soap containers, or for the younger children finger puppets can be made. Plastic Meccano, Playplax, and Kugeli are useful items for making space stations.

Paintings and individual collages of lift-offs, splash-downs, journeys in space, astronauts and satellites, can be a varied and interesting activity for all the children.

The collages can be made from fabric, paper, polystyrene, plastic, string, ribbon, bottle tops and foil. Natural objects such as shells, small stones, seeds and grasses can also be used.

Mathematics
The children can measure large spaces such as the hall, playground and corridor. A variety of methods can be used according to their development, e.g. trundle wheels, measuring sticks, paces, footprints. Desk surfaces can be covered with cardboard or plastic shapes. Involve the children in work on tessellation.

Social Studies

Remind the children of the area where a splash-down usually takes place – The South Pacific, and the many islands in that part of the world. What are the people like who live on these islands?

The First Man in Space – Yuri Gagarin. This was an historic journey. Since then the first men have landed on the Moon from the Apollo 11 Mission. These men showed great courage. Before them other men (and women) have shown great courage by going to places unknown to them.

Mention can then be made of people such as David Livingstone, Captain Speke, Edward Whymper, Sir Edmund Hillary and Sherpa Tensing, Amy Johnson, Gladys Aylward.

Religious Education

BIBLICAL MATERIAL

It is very wonderful that God made the heavens as well as the earth. The glory of God shown in the heavens (Psalm 19: 1). The making of the heavens (Genesis 1: 6).

PRAYERS: A prayer for astronauts is to be found in *Please God* by Beryl Bye and Joyce Badrocke (Church Pastoral Aid Society). Children can also write their own prayers.

HYMNS

Space-men are ready (From *New Child Songs* – Denholm House Press)

Lord, I love to stamp and shout (relevant verses) – (From *New Songs for the Church* – Galliard)

Here are new words for 'All things bright and beautiful' (by A. J. Beeson, reproduced by permission):

> With telescopes and radar
> We look out into space;
> And wonder how the stars there
> Are all kept in their place.
>
> *Chorus: All things bright and beautiful*
>
> We try as hard as ever
> To understand the plan
> That holds the skies together;
> But, Oh! it's hard for man!

Chorus: All things bright and beautiful

For what we know already
And all that is in store,
We thank the Lord of all things
And love Him all the more.

Chorus: All things bright and beautiful

ASSEMBLY A Festival of Space Travel or Lord of Space will be suitable titles for the work which will have been done.

Further Source Material

FILMSTRIPS

(for the older children) *Wonders of God's Universe* *Getting to know God through His World* (selected frames) } (Concordia Films)

TRANSPARENCIES: A set of nine *First Men on the Moon – Apollo 11* series MNO1 is available from Woodmansterne Ltd. Reproductions of the Apollo 15 Mission are also available.

Other suitable transparencies are obtainable from the Royal Astronomical Society. The various Missionary Societies should be able to provide transparencies or filmstrips on work in the South Pacific.

WALL PICTURE: *God gives me the night* from *Present Day picture set* by Frances Hook (from National Christian Education Council)

REFERENCE BOOKS

'*They were First*' series:
Gagarin: Bleriot
Whymper: Hillary and Tensing } by D. Newton and D. Smith
Johnson: Earhart } (Oliver & Boyd)
Speke: La Salle

'Rockets and Satellites' (*Let's Read and Find Out Books*) by F. M. Branley (A. & C. Black)
The Junior True Book of Space by I. Podendorf (Muller)
I want to be a Space Pilot by C. Greene (W. & R. Chambers)
The Astronaut ('*What do they do*' series) by M. Pollard (Macmillan)

3. Sun, Moon and Stars

Starting Point
This section will best follow SPACE as attention can be focussed on the heavenly bodies which we know about through everyday life.

Language Development
Landings on the Moon will have been mentioned in the Space section. These can be re-called and the importance of the moon and stars at night, and the sun by day, talked about with the children.

SUGGESTIONS FOR CREATIVE WRITING
A Visit to a Star
What I found on the Moon

STORIES TO BE READ OR TOLD
'*The Sun that shone too much*' by Denis Wrigley (Wheaton)
'*The Sun looks down*' by Miriam Schlein (Abelard-Schuman)
'*Sun Up*' by Alvin Tressel (World's Work)
'*The Moon Princess*' by David Bolt (Paul Hamlyn)
'*Nigel on a Star*' from *Stories for all Seasons* (National Christian Education Council)

POETRY
The Moon by R. L. Stevenson from *Poetry and Life* (Schofield & Sims)
Stars by Rhoda W. Bacmeister from *More Poems to read to the very young* selected by Josette Frank (Odhams)
The Night Sky – poet unknown from *Poetry Panorama, Book 2* (Odhams)
Sun and Moon by Charlotte Druitt Cole from *Come Follow Me – poems for the very young* (Evans)
Escape at Bedtime by R. L. Stevenson from *The Swinging Rainbow – poems for the young* selected by Howard Sergeant (Evans)

Art and Craft
Mobiles can be made from Artstraws and hung against a

dark blue or black background. Individual pictures using a background of paint, but with various other textures for the sun, moon and stars are very effective. A collage of the heavens can also be made on a wall panel.

Science
The children can be encouraged to go into their gardens, or if this is not possible, to go with parents to a convenient place outside their homes, to view the night sky. According to the time of year indicate where to look in the sky for well known constellations such as The Plough, Orion's Belt, and so on.

Children who live close to London may be able to visit the Planetarium.

Religious Education
BIBLICAL MATERIAL
The sun, moon and stars were created (Genesis 1: 14–18, Psalm 74: 16)
We read about the sun and the moon (Psalms 89: 37, 104: 19, and 121: 6)
The star which was shining brightly on the night that Jesus was born (Matthew 2: 2, 9)

PRAYERS: After the children have been able to view the moon and the stars from their homes they will be ready to talk about what they have seen. It will be good to gain their impressions. Prayers of thanks for the wonder of the heavens can then be spoken or written.
Dear God, Maker of all things, we want to remember all the things we like about the moon and stars (let the children say) .... For them all we say, Thank You, God. Amen
(from *Praying With Primaries* by Dorothy Wilton – National Christian Education Council)
Other suitable prayers are to be found in this publication, and *Time* and *Again Prayers* (O.U.P.)

HYMNS
Sun and Moon and Stars of Heaven (From *The Morning Cockerel Hymnbook*, Rupert Hart-Davis)

Every Star shall sing a Carol (From *Faith, Folk and Clarity*, Galliard)

The Star (From *Sing a New Song* by Bridget Ball, Religious Education Press)

I Love the Sun (relevant verses)

God who made the earth (verses 1 and 3) } *New Child Songs*
Look up! Look up! See the stars in space } (Denholm House Press)

Here is a new hymn which can be sung to the tune *Easter Alleluia*:

> All round the world young voices sing,
> Praising the name of Christ our King,
>   Alleluia, Alleluia.
> From distant islands comes the call
> God is the Father of us all!
>   O praise Him, Alleluia,
> Alleluia, Alleluia, Alleluia.
>
> Earth, planets, stars that swing in space
> Echo with praise from every race,
>   Alleluia, Alleluia.
> Christ is our King, let all proclaim,
> Tell all the world in His great name,
>   And praise Him, Alleluia,
> Alleluia, Alleluia, Alleluia.

ASSEMBLY: Centre an Assembly around the work which has been done. A suitable title is 'Wonder of the Heavens'. As an alternative, the children may like to use 'Lord of the Heavens', or suggest titles themselves.

Further Source Material
FILMSTRIPS

The Mighty Hunters (Concordia Films)
Discoveries in God's World – selected frames for the older children (National Christian Education Council)

PRINT
Fishermen in Sunset (Athena Reproductions Ltd.)

WALL PICTURE: *God gives me the night* (From *Present Day Picture Set* by Frances Hook, from National Christian Education Council)

REFERENCE BOOKS

What the Moon is like ⎱
The Sun: Our nearest Star ⎰ 'Let's Read and Find Out Books'
by F. M. Branley
The Moon seems to change ⎰ (A. & C. Black)

Sunshine and Shadow – 'Things I Like' series by Peggy Blakeley (A. & C. Black)

Moon ⎱
Sun ⎰ Macdonald Starters (MacDonald Educational)

Man needs the Sun by S. C. George – *Star Book series* (Hamish Hamilton)

We Discover – Sun, Moon and Stars by R. H. C. Fice and I. M. Simkiss (E. J. Arnold)

4. Daytime and Night Time

Starting Point

Talk with the children about their activities of the previous evening. Night came and they went to bed. Discuss the playtime which they enjoyed before going to bed, and stories which may have been read by them or told by a parent. After a night's sleep the new day dawned, and the activities of another day started.

Language Development

SUGGESTIONS FOR CREATIVE WRITING
What is Night Time?
What is Daytime?
I like to dream about . . .
My most wonderful day

Teachers can commence a story orally about the time when the toys came to life after everyone had gone to sleep. The children can finish it.

STORIES TO BE READ OR TOLD
'When the lights went out' – *Stories for all seasons* (National Christian Education Council)
Nutcracker and Mouse King (E. T. A. Hoffmann) – consult your local Library.
Selections from *365 Goodnight Stories* (Paul Hamlyn)

POETRY

Bedtime
Woolly Blanket } by Kate Cox Goddard from *More Poems to read to the very young* selected by Josette Frank (Odhams)

Singing Time by Rose Fyleman
Time to Rise by R. L. Stevenson from *A Child's Garden of Verse* (Collins)
The Night Sky – poet unknown from *Poetry Panorama, Book 2* (Odhams)

Pippa's Song by Robert Browning
Good Night by Victor Hugo } From *Come Follow Me* – *poems for the very young* (Evans)

Bed in Summer by R. L. Stevenson from *The Swinging Rainbow* – *poems for the young* selected by Howard Sergeant (Evans)

Days – part of a poem by Philip Larkin
Early in the Morning by Charles Causley

} *From Bits and Pieces* – *poems for young readers* chosen by Peggy Blakeley (A. & C. Black)

Art and Craft
Wax resist pictures of night time can be made and placed close to paintings of daytime. See *Let's Make Pictures* by H. Pluckrose (Mills and Boon)

Daytime and Night time collages can also be made using a variety of scrap materials. Eastern type oil lamps can be made using clay and candles.

Mathematics
Block Graphs can be made of the times that the children go to bed, and also the time when they get up in the morning.

Music
Clair de Lune – Debussy, SXL 2293 (Decca)
The Nutcracker Suite – Tchaikovsky, SXL 2092-3 (Decca)

Religious Education
BIBLICAL MATERIAL
God called the light day, and the darkness night (Genesis 1: 5)
While the earth lasts ... day and night shall never cease (Genesis 8: 22)
God made two great lights, the sun to rule by day and the moon by night (Genesis 1: 16–18 and Psalm 136: 7–9)
Time to lay down peacefully and sleep (Psalm 4: 8)
A busy day in the life of Jesus (Mark 1: 21–34)

PRAYERS: It may well be right to remember that some children have problems about night time and the darkness. Discussion about this part of the day, and prayers, may need to be dealt with carefully.

The children can talk about, and write, the prayers they

25

would like to say at night, and at the beginning of each new day.

Suitable prayers can be found in *Praying with Primaries* by Dorothy Wilton, and *Praying with Juniors* by Jack and Edna Young (National Christian Education Council)

Some of the hymns listed below are also suitable as prayers.

HYMNS

A Prayer ⎱ from *Sing a New Song* by Bridget Ball (Religious
Evensong ⎰ Education Press)

Father, we thank Thee for the night   ⎱ From *The Morning Cockerel Hymnbook* (Rupert Hart-Davis)
The Lights go up all over the town
The golden cockerel crows in the morning

I love the day-time ⎱ from *New Child Songs* (Denholm
What makes the daytime ⎰ House Press)

Further Source Material

FILMSTRIP: for the younger children. *God cares through a dependable world* (selected frames) (National Christian Education Council)

WALL PICTURES

Bedtime from *Life in Bible Times Picture Set* by Wilbur Adam
Now I lay me down to sleep ⎱ From *Present Day Picture Set* by
God gives me the night ⎰ Frances Hook
Talking With Mummy ⎱ From *Friends Picture Set* by
Friends from Everywhere ⎰ Frances Hook
The above Picture Sets are available from the National Christian Education Council

REFERENCE BOOKS

Night – MacDonald Starter (MacDonald Educational)
Night by Althea (Souvenir Press Ltd.)

5. Water

Starting Point

Although our children are familiar with water it will help to make them think how easily we get it for drinking, washing and cooking.

Let the children have a drink of water from the water fountain, the tap, or if more convenient from a small beaker or yoghourt container which they can use whilst sitting at their tables or desks.

Have a supply of items whereby water is needed, e.g. a saucepan for cooking vegetables; a piece of soap and a flannel; toothbrush and toothpaste; a vase of flowers, and seeds to be sown.

Language Development

How easily we get our water! This statement can be used to draw reactions from the children, and lead further into the various uses of water. The uses can be listed on the blackboard, and at a later stage written down by the children in a Work Book.

SUGGESTIONS FOR CREATIVE WRITING
News item on how the children use water
Bath-time
The bath that went to sea

STORIES TO BE READ OR TOLD
'Topsy and Tim's Paddling Pool' by Jean and Gareth Adamson (Blackie)
'The Water Babies' by Charles Kingsley – *Favourite series* (Nelson)
'When the floods came' – *Stories for all Seasons* (National Christian Education Council)
'I'm Thirsty' – *Getting to know Botswana* (Christian Education Movement)

POETRY
The Rain by R. L. Stevenson from *Happy Landings – poems for the youngest* chosen by Howard Sergeant (Evans)

Water by John R. Crossland ⎱ From *Come Follow Me – poems*
The Rain by W. H. Davies ⎰ *for the very young* (Evans)
A Wet Day by Mary Daunt from *Passport to Poetry Book 1*
edited by E. L. Black & D. S. Davies (Cassell)
Water Lilies by John Clare from *The Patchwork Quilt and
Other Poems* selected by Joan Cass (Longmans)

Art and Craft

The children can produce their own paintings of the everyday uses of water, e.g. washing, bath-time, watering the
indoor plants. When the paintings are finished have a discussion about them and let the children give each one a title.
A 'Gallery of Water Paintings' can then be established in a
corridor or a part of the hall.

Science

Various experiments can be carried out and discoveries made
about
   (*a*) Objects which float or sink
   (*b*) Some materials which dry more quickly than others
   (*c*) Weigh items such as a sponge and various thicknesses
       of material, both wet and dry. What is the difference?
   (*d*) Watch coloured water ascend a flower stalk.

Mathematics

Capacity work using a variety of unmarked containers. The
children can then progress to metric containers.

Social Studies

Because water is so common to us the children will not
realize that it is scarce in some parts of the world. One of the
countries which suffers from drought is Botswana. The leaflet
Getting to know Botswana from the Christian Education Movement will be helpful. Also, visual material from Christian
Aid and Save the Children of the work which they do in
various parts of the world.

Music

Water Music, Handel, ASD 577 (EMI)
Blue Danube, Strauss, SXL 6029 (Decca)

28

P.E. and Movement

Let the children act a scene which would have been a common sight in an Eastern village when Jesus was alive. The women gather at the well to draw water and talk to each other. The children can work in groups as villagers talking; others can be drawing water, and individuals can pretend to carry the filled water pots on their shoulders.

Another session can involve the children as seeds asleep in the soft, warm earth; as raindrops, and the warm sun. The seeds are awakened by the rain and the sun, and growth starts. There can be a period without rain when the plants wilt. Later it rains again and the plants grow strong.

Religious Education

BIBLICAL MATERIAL

Jesus sometimes rested by a well (John 4: 3–6)
Jesus talking to a lady by the well (John 4: 7)
Clouds gather in the sky and the rain comes (Psalm 147: 8)
In cold weather there is ice, the water becomes frozen, and when the wind blows hard the water in the rivers and streams melts and flows swiftly (Psalm 147: 17–18)
Water flows in the valleys (Psalm 104: 10)
Water was very precious and a song was once sung about it (Numbers 21: 17–18)

PRAYERS: Use the prayer entitled 'Rain' by Dorothy R. Wilton from *Praying With Primaries* (National Christian Education Council). The children can then write their own prayers of thanks for water. These can be placed alongside the paintings which will have been done previously.

Talk about the kind of prayer the children will want to use for people who have no water. This activity could take place after the children have listened to the story 'I'm Thirsty'.

HYMNS

The Rain Hymn from *Sing a New Song* by Bridget Ball (Religious Education Press)
When I needed a neighbour (relevant verses) *from Faith, Folk and Clarity* (Galliard)

Raindrops } *New Child Songs* (Denholm House
God sends the water } Press)

ASSEMBLY: A Harvest of Water

Further Source Material

FILMSTRIPS

We Enjoy God's Gifts (selected frames), (National Christian
Education Council)

Playing in the Rain (for the younger children) }
Discoveries in God's World (selected frames for the } (Concordia
older children) } Films)

WALL PICTURES

God sends the Rain (From the Present Day Picture Set)
Friends from Everywhere (From the Friends Picture Set)
Both by Frances Hook (from National Christian Education
Council)

REFERENCE BOOKS

Water – MacDonald First Library (MacDonald Educational)
Rain – MacDonald Starter (MacDonald Educational)
Water all around us by T. S. Pine and J. Levine (Blackie)
The People and Lands of the Bible by R. W. Thomson (Hulton)
The Land Where Jesus Lived, Book 3, by E. R. Boyce (Macmillan)
Water appears and disappears by G. O. Blough (Wheaton)
Water by Althea (Souvenir Press Ltd.)

6. The Seaside

Starting Point

This section can conveniently follow on from Water. It can be a natural follow-up as to the way in which water provides pleasure at the seaside. It will be good to stress the importance of sensible behaviour as the sea can be dangerous as well as a place for fun.

Environmental Visit

If it is possible take the children to the beach. As an alternative, the children can view visual aids, e.g. pictures, transparencies.

Language Development

Many children will have been to the seaside, and others will have some idea of what it is like through scenes of the sea which they will have viewed on the television. Talk with them about the different things to be seen, and if a visit has been made, discuss the items which can be found on a beach.

SUGGESTIONS FOR CREATIVE WRITING

The Sea Creature's Palace
Treasures in the Sand
A Walk on the beach
A news story can also be written about a visit, whether with the school, or with parents if this was a recent experience.

STORIES TO BE READ OR TOLD

'*Little Tim and the Brave Sea Captain*' ⎫
'*Tim to the Rescue*' ⎬ by Edward Ardizzone
'*Tim and Lucy go to Sea*' ⎭ (O.U.P.)

Little Tim and the Brave Sea Captain is also available as a film-strip from Weston Woods Studios Ltd.

'Happy Holidays' ⎫ From *Stories for all Seasons*
'It sometimes rains on Summer ⎬ (National Christian
Days' ⎭ Education Council)

POETRY

At the Seaside by R. L. Stevenson from *First Poems,* Book *1*

The Horses of the Sea by Christina Rossetti from *First Poems, Book 2* — Schofield & Sims

Wild are the Waves by Walter de la Mare from *First Poems, Book 3*

There are big waves by Eleanor Farjeon from *Five, Sixes and Sevens* (Warne)

I'd like to be a Lighthouse by Rachel Field from *A Penny Wish* (E. J. Arnold)

White Horses by Irene F. Pawsey (the reading of the poem may well be linked with the suggestion for Creative Writing – The Sea Creature's Palace

Castles in the Sand by Dorothy Baker. These last two poems are from *Come Follow Me – poems for the very young* (Evans)

Art and Craft

The children can make a collage of the Seaside in which a variety of materials and textures are used to show the sand, cliffs, boats on the sea, a lighthouse and children playing happily with their families.

Mosaics can be made from small pebbles and broken shells.

Model boats and lighthouses will be a helpful activity. An interesting wall design will be that of the Sea Creature's Palace, using blue and green tissue paper, and well washed seaweed to suggest the sea washing over the palace.

Social Studies

A valuable part of such a section as this is the teaching which can be given about the dangers of the seaside as well as the pleasures. The children can be encouraged to learn to swim in the local swimming baths, or to use the facilities available at local schools. The dangers of floating air beds and rubber dinghies when playing at the seaside can be emphasized.

The Royal Society for the Prevention of Accidents will provide material, e.g. The Water Safety Code.

Music

Noyes Fludde by Benjamin Britten ZNF 1. Excerpts, especially the rendering of 'Eternal Father', could be a highlight of the section.

P.E. and Movement

The children can imagine that they are going for a walk on the beach. They will feel the sand trickling through their toes; the cool water as the sea comes up and laps around their feet; the warmer water of the little rock pools. They will feel the slimy seaweed, and jump over pieces of driftwood and then come suddenly upon the Sea Creature's Palace. From this point their own imagination takes over as they enter the strange world of the Sea Creature.

Religious Education

BIBLICAL MATERIAL: Many instances of the times that Jesus spent around the shores of Lake Galilee can be found in the Gospels, e.g. The lakeside at Galilee and the fishermen Jesus knew (Mark 1 : 16–20).

PRAYERS

> For the sand on the beach,
> For the gulls on the cliff,
> For the slow river's reach,
> For the salt sea's whiff,
> We thank Thee, heavenly Father.

(from *Praying With Juniors* by Jack and Edna Young – National Christian Education Council)

HYMNS

In Galilee beside the Sea
Sea Song from *Sing a New Song* by Bridget Ball (Religious Education Press)
What fun it is beside the sea ⎫ From *New Child Songs*
Thank You, God, for lovely sea ⎭ (Denholm House Press)

ASSEMBLY: Thank You, Lord God, for the Seaside.

Further Source Material

FILMSTRIPS

Enjoying Our Holiday (for the older children) – (National Christian Education Council)

Life on the Sea-Shore (Educational Productions)

TRANSPARENCIES: These may be supplied by children and teachers who have spent a holiday at the seaside.

REFERENCE BOOKS

Underwater Exploration (Ladybird)

By the Sea – MacDonald First Library (MacDonald Educational)

The Sea
Seashore } MacDonald Starters (MacDonald Educational)

Seaside Treasures (Mills & Boon)

THEME TWO

NATURE

1. **All Sorts of Flowers**

2. **Birds**

3. **Trees**

4. **Animals**

5. **Colour**

1. All Sorts of Flowers

Starting Point
The children can be asked to bring flowers from their gardens or, if this is not possible their teacher can bring as large a variety as possible. Try to gather enough so that groups can make their own flower arrangement.

Environmental Visit
Try to visit a local park or beauty spot where flowers can be seen growing to advantage. If a local church is presenting a Festival of Flowers this will provide an ideal visit.

Language Development
Encourage the children to talk about the different flowers in their arrangements. What are the names of the flowers? Where did they come from? Do they have different shapes? Are they different in colour? Develop the aspect of wonder at their beauty, and the care which has been shown in growing them.

News items, both oral and written, can be a follow-up to the Environmental Visit.

SUGGESTIONS FOR CREATIVE WRITING

My Beautiful Flower Garden
Fairyland Flowers
Moon Flowers

STORIES TO BE READ OR TOLD

'Beryl's Flower Service'
'The Little Gardeners'
} From *Stories for All Seasons* (National Christian Education Council)

POETRY

Violets by Mary Webb
Snowdrops by Mary Vivian
The Forget-Me-Not – Poet Unknown
Crocuses by Anna M. Platt
Marigolds by Louis Driscoll
} From *Come Follow Me – Poems for the very young* (Evans)

Window-Boxes by Eleanor Farjeon from *Poetry Panorama 2* (Odhams Books).

Art and Craft

The Flower arrangements can be displayed on 'Our Table of Beautiful Flowers'. Large yellow sunflowers can be made by using Finart Finger Paint. Crinkled tissue or crepe paper, coloured gummed paper, and material from the scrap box will all be useful for making a collage. Centres of egg boxes will give a 3D effect for flowers with trumpets.

A frieze of Holy Land Flowers can be made with pictures from the Holy Lands Bible Society. Old Christmas cards can also be helpful in work of this nature. Flower and seed catalogues can provide material for decorating children's individual or group work books. 'My Book of Flowers' can contain news, creative writing, prayers, poems and some forms of art work.

Fabricrayon from Finart will also help the children to produce brightly coloured flowers.

Towers of flowers can be made by covering cardboard tubes in good quality paper, and then pinning on flower shapes which have been made using various techniques, e.g. rosettes, tissue paper overlay, Fabricrayon.

Effective flowers can also be made from coloured tissues and soft toilet paper.

Science

Work can be carried out on how flowers grow. Perhaps a miniature garden can be established. Children can observe and record daily findings on the growth of seeds which germinate quickly.

Social Studies

Develop interest in flowers which are grown in other lands. Visual Aids will be invaluable here, as the children will need to see what the flowers look like. Perhaps it can be arranged for the children to see pictures or transparencies of the gentian from Switzerland, and bougainvillea from the West Indies. Travel Agents and the Tourist Departments of Government Offices may be able to provide large posters.

Religious Education

Conservation and caring for the flowers in the hedgerows as

well as gardens should provide a central learning point for this section of the Nature theme.

BIBLICAL MATERIAL

Sometimes wealthy people grew plants in their gardens, e.g. mustard (Luke 13: 19)

The lilies of the fields (Matthew 6: 28)

King Ahab asks Naboth if he can have his vineyard for a garden (I Kings 21: 1–2). Vineyards were sometimes tended by people who would have treated them like gardens.

For now the winter is past,
the rains are over and gone;
the flowers appear in the country-side (Song of Solomon or Songs 2: 11–12)

PRAYERS

> Colourful flowers,
> Sweet smelling flowers,
> Some with large petals,
> Others so small and delicate.
> For all this beauty,
> We say 'Thank You, Father God.'

For this prayer it will be best used if the children sit in a relaxed manner with their eyes open and focussed upon a flower arrangement.

Prayers of thanks, and caring for garden and wild flowers can be written and placed on 'Our Table of Beautiful Flowers'. Prayers can also be integrated with frieze and collage work when it is placed around the room.

HYMNS

Seeds and bulbs are all asleep (relevant verses) from *New Child Songs* (Denholm House Press)

My Garden (From *Sing a New Song* by Bridget Ball, Religious Education Press)

A Secret Flower ⎱ From *The Morning Cockerel Hymnbook*
Praised be our Lord ⎰ (Rupert Hart-Davis)

Daisies are our silver

To God who made all lovely things

ASSEMBLY: Make arrangements for the Hall to be well

38

decorated with various kinds of flowers. For this occasion other classes can be asked to contribute. Perhaps parents with a flair for flower arrangement would welcome the opportunity to assist in this activity. Children's work, and new hymns learned will be a part of the Assembly, but the order of proceedings can only be decided by the teacher(s) involved. However, after the Assembly the flowers could be distributed to a local Old People's Home, the hospital, or other deserving causes known to teachers in their own local situations.

Further Source Material

FILMSTRIP (for the younger children)

Surprise from Concordia Films

TRANSPARENCIES

The Pots of Flowers – Cézanne
Bouquet des Fleurs – Gauguin
Sunflowers – Van Gogh
Mixed Flowers in a Vase – Van Gogh

From the National Gallery Publications Department

WALL PICTURES

A Vineyard from *Life in Bible Times Picture Set* by Wilbur Adams (from National Christian Education Council)
Large wall pictures from seed and bulb catalogues

REFERENCE BOOKS

Garden Flowers (Ladybird)
Animals, Birds and Plants of the Bible (Ladybird)
How Flowers Live – *MacDonald First Library* (MacDonald Educational)
The Flower, by Althea (Souvenir Press Ltd.)
Concrete Yard Gardening – an account of work with very young children by Nancy J. Quayle (School Natural Science Society)

2. Birds

Starting Point

This section can be started in various ways; therefore teachers may like to select one of the following methods:

1. Transparencies can be shown of various British wild and domestic birds. These can be obtained from the Royal Society for the Protection of Birds.

2. Visit a Bird Sanctuary, or the relevant section of a park or zoo.

3. A pet bird may be brought to school.

Language Development

The children will want to talk about their experiences and enjoyment according to whichever of the above methods is selected as a Starting Point. Conversation will flow easily in regard to their likes and dislikes. Which birds would make favourite pets? Which birds did they enjoy watching? If a mynah bird was present in the Sanctuary or Zoo it was probably the cause of much fun.

The children can report orally and in writing about their visit. Other written work can include items such as:

The Magic Bird Garden
The bird who talked too much
What is a bird?
Who lives in the nest in my garden?
A news story about a bird which is kept as a pet.

STORIES TO BE READ OR TOLD
'*The tale of the Little Brown Bird*' by Elizabeth Clark from *Time for a Story* (Penguin)
'*The Nestling*' from *Starlight and Sunshine* (Schofield & Sims)
'*Beaky the Greedy Duck*' by Noel Barr (Ladybird)
'*The Little Sparrow*' by Frances Eager (Hamish Hamilton)
'*How the Nightingale got its Voice*' by Margaret Goodland – Glow-worm series (E. J. Arnold)
'*The Sparrows and the Market Place*' from *Jesus, Friend of Birds and Beasts* (R.E.P.)

40

'*The Crowing Cock*' by H. G. Moses (E. J. Arnold and Denholm House Press)
'*The Chicken and the Egg*' from '*All God's Children*' by Pauline M. Webb (Oliphants)

POETRY

Nest Eggs by R. L. Stevenson from *A Child's Garden of Verse* (Collins)
The Blackbird by Humbert Wolfe from *Bits and Pieces – Poems for young readers* chosen by Peggy Blakeley (A. & C. Black)

Birds' Nests by Millicent Seager
The Eagle by Lord Tennyson
Kindness to Animals – Poet Unknown
The Nightingale by Katharine Tynan
Robin's Song by Rodney Bennett
The Bird Bath by Florence Hoatson

From *Come Follow Me – Poems for the very young* (Evans)

Art and Craft

Large individual pictures of birds can be made using a variety of materials and textures, e.g. feathers from feather dusters, coloured net and other bits and pieces from the scrap box, various paper techniques, and Jumbo 'Artstraws'. These can then be incorporated into a wall collage entitled The Bird Garden.

A frieze of birds from overlay pictures, using felt pens or chalk for the overlay technique will be colourful. Also, mathematical gummed paper shapes, e.g. circles, triangles, rectangles and metric strips can be used effectively.

Science

Mount an exhibition of birds' feathers, nests and blown eggs. The aspect of caring for the birds can be developed through this exhibition. Nesting habits, respect for the eggs, and the use of bird tables, can all be covered and the exhibition can be captioned 'We Care for the Birds'. The children can also learn about the unpleasant habits of some birds such as the cuckoo, and how young eagles learn to fly.

Mathematics

If there are a sufficient number of children keeping birds as pets a graph of the different species can be made, or alternatively a graph can be produced showing the popularity of the birds seen on a visit, or from transparencies which may have been shown.

Social Studies
Select a few birds from other countries, e.g. the Lyre Bird from Australia and Flamingoes from South America and provide the children with information about them.

RECORDINGS OF BIRD SOUNDS
The following records will be useful:
Sound effects record SZ 280 from E. J. Arnold contains a dawn chorus.
Fun at the Zoo – Roundabout Series No. 1 B.B.C. (Bands 2 & 4)
A Salute to Ludwig Koch – B.B.C. Wildlife Series No. 1 RED 34M
A Year's Journey – B.B.C. Records

Music and Story
Stories from a ballet – Swan Lake 7EG 112

MOVEMENT SONGS

Swallows
Little Brown Sparrow } From Movement Songs for Infant Classes by Gwendoline E. Holt (Boosey & Hawkes)
The Dovecote from *Twenty Songs for Nursery and Infant Schools* compiled by Winifred E. Houghton (Boosey & Hawkes)

Religious Education
Throughout the development of this section the accent will have been placed on the care and protection of birds thus promoting the aspect of caring.

BIBLICAL MATERIAL: Birds of the bible can be talked about and described. When possible link the material with birds seen and known about today.
God cares for the sparrows (Luke 12: 6)
The Swallow (Psalm 84: 3)

The Dove (Genesis 8: 8–9)
The Raven (I Kings 17: 4. Also, the fine glossy black plumage of the raven is mentioned in Song of Solomon *or* Songs 5: 11)
The Eagle (Deuteronomy 32: 11. Mention is made of the place and height of eagle's nest in Jeremiah 49: 16)

PRAYERS: The children can make their own prayers of thanks for birds which they have as pets; those which they may see on the way to school, and other wild birds. If it is possible to hear birds whilst learning is in progress the following prayer may be used at any time:

> Listen!
> Let's be still.
> Chattering, chirping, singing birds.
> Thank You, God for this time,
> And every happy thing.

Also, if a pet bird is brought to school, talk about the delicate appearance of its legs and claws; the texture of its feathers, the shape of its head, and other items which the children will mention. Then with attention focussed on the bird, the children can keep their eyes open whilst a prayer of thanks is spoken by the teacher.

HYMNS
Praise Him, sang the Blackbird (From *Sing a New Song* by Bridget Ball, R.E.P.)

The Golden Cockerel crows in the morning
A Secret Bird (Verse 2 of 'A Secret Flower') } From *The Morning Cockerel Hymn-book* (Rupert Hart-Davis)

All things which live below the sky (relevant verses)
I Love the Birds (verse 6 of ' I Love the Sun' – *Infant Praise* (O.U.P.)
In the Winter, birds need food (From *New Child Songs* (Denholm House Press)

ASSEMBLY: This could be entitled 'Birds!' 'Beautiful Birds!' or 'We Care for the Birds'. Material from the

43

classroom can be displayed in the Hall and children's work used in the worship time.

Further Source Material

TRANSPARENCIES: Films and other material are available from the Royal Society for the Protection of Birds, and The Wildlife Panda Club.

WALL PICTURES

Pet Budgies from *the Friends Picture Set* } by Frances Hook
God takes care of the birds from the } (from National
Present Day Picture Set } Christian Education
} Council)

REFERENCE BOOKS

British Wild Birds
Garden Birds } (Ladybird)
Animals, Birds and Plants of the Bible }
Birds by Brian Wildsmith (O.U.P.)
We Discover Birds (E. J. Arnold)
Birds – MacDonald Starter (MacDonald Educational)
Observe and Learn – Birds by Mollie Clarke (Rupert Hart-Davis)
Our Bird Friends (First Shelf series W. & R. Chambers Ltd.)
The Longmans Bird Series
All About Creatures on Islands and Things by Althea and published for the National Trust by Dinosaur Publications Ltd.

3. Trees

Starting Point
An Environmental Visit to the local park, or countryside, will be the best point at which to commence this section. Items can be collected according to the season, e.g. leaves, blossom, acorns, conkers, twigs.

Language Development
The children can talk and write about their visit as well as produce their suggestions for creative writing on the following lines:—

The Land beyond the Trees

Lost in the Woods (this can be a continuation of Drama)

The Babes in the Wood – the children re-tell the story in their own words.

STORIES TO BE READ OR TOLD

'The Babes in the Wood'

Robin Hood stories

High Adventure by Ursula Moray Williams (Nelson)

The Great Surprise (The story of Zaccheus – *Arch Book*, Concordia)

POETRY

The Cherry Tree by Walter de la Mare from *Poetry and Life Bk. 1* (Schofield & Sims)

Trees by Sara Coleridge ⎫ From *Come Follow*
Tall Trees by Eileen Mathias ⎬ *Me – poems for the very*
Chestnut Buds by Evelyn M. Williams ⎭ *young* (Evans)

DRAMA: The majority of the children can be trees growing in a wood. The remainder are lost in the wood and become entangled in the branches of various trees which then come alive. Let the children continue the sequence of events.

Art and Craft
A display of items collected from a visit can be arranged in a decorative manner on a Nature Table. Reference books and

45

verses or paraphrases from the Bible can be integrated with the display. A possible passage is Psalm 104: 16–17.

Creative leaf shapes can be made by splashing paint blots on paper which is then folded in half. This can also be linked with symmetry in the Mathematics section.

Leaf and bark rubbings along with leaf prints can be used as a decoration for a class book about trees. Leaves can also be pressed and when they are dry used to make book marks. The pressed leaves can be stuck on to strips of card and covered in a transparent material such as Fablon. If this activity is done in the Autumn it could lead to giving presents to a local Children's or Old People's Home at Christmas.

A collage of trees can be made using a variety of material including Artstraws. Prayers of thanks can be integrated with the art work. A frieze can be made using children's individual pictures and those which are suitable from magazines.

Science

Twigs, bark, leaves, buds and blossom, fruit and even drift-wood, if you live close to the seaside, can be brought for the Nature Table. Make sure that it is kept tidy and that specimens are clearly marked. Care of the Nature Table is important as this will encourage the idea of caring for trees, and other natural objects.

Mathematics

Leaves can be arranged in sets according to shape, size and colour. After the preliminary sorting has been done the children can then sort the leaves into those of the same shape and colour, and those of the same size and colour thus leading them into the work which can be done using Logi-blocs.

The children can draw round the leaves on squared paper, and count the squares to find the area. Older children can use squared centimetre paper. Fractions can be introduced with large leaf shapes as the children can draw round them and divide the shape into $\frac{1}{2}$'s and $\frac{1}{4}$'s. Also, look for symmetry in leaf shapes.

Social Studies
Select various types of tree from other lands, e.g. the Douglas Firs from Canada, the Giant Redwoods of California, and the spruce trees from Norway.

Music
Tales from the Vienna Woods – J. Strauss, SXSP 30060
Woods and Fields (Smetana)

P.E. and Movement
The accent can be on body awareness in small and large movements. The children can start by being curled up small and then gradually grow into trees, with branches spreading out. This can be linked with the Drama.

An emphasis can be placed on the texture of different leaves and the children can move as follows: prickly, spiky movements for holly leaves; floating movements for the Autumn time, and expansive, floppy movements for plane leaves, willows and palms.

Religious Education
This is another section in which the children can be brought to appreciate the beauty to be found in the world. This beauty needs to be conserved, and so caring forms an important part of the learning process.

BIBLICAL MATERIAL
Green leafy trees (Psalm 104: 16–17)
The Olive tree (Genesis 8:11)
The king's head anointed with olive oil (1 Samuel 16: 13)
Wood from the olive tree was used in Solomon's Temple (1 Kings 6: 31–32)
Palm branches strewn on the roads on Palm Sunday (Matthew 21: 8)
Jesus watched Joseph use wood in the carpenter's shop.

PRAYERS
There's a (insert name) tree at the bottom of our playground, Lord (or substitute suitable location)
I often wonder

When I look at it
How the leaves are formed, and the tough bark too.
And to think it came from
A seed (beech nut, acorn)
Lord God, I am glad that tree is there!
The children can write their own prayers for the beauty and majesty of trees; the colours of the leaves in the Autumn and their freshness in the Spring.

HYMNS

Palm trees waving against the sky ⎱ From *Sing a New Song*
Sing a song of Springtime ⎰ by Bridget Ball (R.E.P.)
Autumn Leaves (O lovely world of colour) from *New Child Songs* (Denholm House Press)

ASSEMBLY: Collage and frieze work can be taken to the hall for this occasion. Some very tall trees can have been painted or made from coloured gummed paper to provide the setting for The Tall Trees in the Greenwood.

Further Source Material

TRANSPARENCY: *Fruit Trees in blossom* – Van Gogh (The National Gallery)

WALL PICTURES

Zaccheus, come down ⎱ From the *Jesus Picture Set* by
Hosanna to the Son of David ⎰ Frances Hook (from National Christian Education Council)

REFERENCE BOOKS

Trees and Wood – MacDonald First Library (MacDonald Educational)
Trees – MacDonald Starter (MacDonald Educational)
A Tree is a Plant (A. & C. Black)
Lumberjacks by O. B. Gregory (Wheaton)
Little Boy Jesus at Home by M. Redington-White (Brockhampton)
All About Pines and Oaks and Things by Althea and published for the National Trust by Dinosaur Publications Ltd.

48

4. Animals

Starting Point
One of the best methods for starting this section would be a visit to a Zoo, or Animal Sanctuary. As this is not possible for everyone, suitable transparencies or large pictures of various animals can be used to stimulate an interest.

Language Development
The children will talk freely about their visit, or the visual aids which they have seen. The names of various animals, and particularly the rare ones can be listed on large pieces of card. These can be used by groups of children as the work is developed.

Written work can include the following:
Report of a visit to a Zoo or Sanctuary
All About my Pet

SUGGESTIONS FOR CREATIVE WRITING
The Monkeys' Tea Party
The Animals which live in the Little Wood

STORIES TO BE READ OR TOLD:
Ned, the Lonely Donkey }
The Discontented Pony } by Noel Barr (Ladybird)
A Dog so small by Phillipa Pearce (Puffin)
Stephen and the Shaggy Dog by Elizabeth Beresford (Methuen)
The Lion Cub by Eilis Dillon (Hamish Hamilton)

Selections from Adventures in the Little Wood } by Anne-Marie
Selections from Tales of the Little Wood } Dalmais
} (Paul Hamlyn)

St. Francis and the Wolf
Beatrix Potter stories narrated by Vivien Leigh – SZ 329–335 (E. J. Arnold)

POETRY
The Camel's Hump by Rudyard Kipling from *Passport to Poetry, Book 2*, edited by E. L. Black & D. S. Davies (Cassell & Co. Ltd.)

At the Zoo by A. A. Milne from *More Poems to read to the very young* by Josette Frank (Odhams)

The Rabbit by Edith King
Mr. Squirrel by V. M. Julian } From *Come Follow Me*
The Elephant by Herbert Asquith } *poems for the very young*
Prayer for gentleness to all creatures by } (Evans)
John Galsworthy }

Art and Craft

The children can draw round templates of wild animals and colour the shapes with wax crayons. The pictures can then be made into a frieze. Clay models of jungle animals can be made for a Jungle Display. A background for the display can be made up of wax crayon resist pictures using a stain to highlight effect. Stick prints using rubber foam or polystyrene will also provide interesting animal pictures.

Social Studies

The wild animals of the African continent will provide a rich variety of learning material for the children. Large pictures can be obtained from Travel Agents and the Government and Tourist Offices of the relevant countries.

Music and Records

Carnival of the Animals narrated by Michael Flanders, SZ 233 (E. J. Arnold) or HMV ASD 2753 or CSD 1624
Fun at the Zoo – Roundabout Series No. 1, B.B.C.
Peter and the Wolf

MOVEMENT SONGS
The Zoo from *Movement Songs for Infant Classes* by Gwendoline E. Holt (Boosey & Hawkes)
Platypus Song from *Willy-Wally Walkabout* (Boosey & Hawkes)

Religious Education

BIBLICAL MATERIAL
Abraham owned sheep, cattle, asses and camels (Genesis 12: 16)
Tents were made from the hair of many goats, also rams' skins (Exodus 36: 14–19)

Donkeys were loaded with food which was taken to David (I Samuel 25: 18-20)
Mountain goats and rock badgers (conies) are mentioned in Psalm 104: 18
Beasts of the forests and young lions (Psalm 104: 20-21)
John the Baptist wore a coat made from camel hair (Matthew 3: 4)
Jesus knew that foxes roamed the countryside (Matthew 8: 20)
Jesus rode into Jerusalem on a donkey (Matthew 21: 1-11).
The shepherds were guarding their sheep when Jesus was born (Luke 2: 8)

PRAYERS: Thank you prayers for the various animals which the children have learned about, e.g. the chattering monkeys, the tall giraffe. It will also be helpful to use selections from *Praying with Primaries* by Dorothy R. Wilton (National Christian Education Council); *Please God* by Beryl Bye and Joyce Badrocke (Church Pastoral Aid Society); and *Time and Again Prayers* compiled by Janet Cookson and Margaret Rogers (O.U.P.).

HYMNS
The King of Love
The Animals } From *Sing a New Song* by Bridget Ball (R.E.P.)
The Camels

I Love God's tiny creatures } From *The Morning Cockerel Hymnbook* (Rupert Hart-Davis)
All things which live below the sky

All creatures of our God and King } From *New Child Songs* (Denholm House Press)
Praise be to God for His creatures wild (verse 3 of Country Life)

ASSEMBLY The work can be brought to a climax with an Assembly entitled: Be kind to all the Animals *or* All creatures of our God and King.

Further Source Material
TRANSPARENCIES
The Learning about Animals series (Encyclopaedia Britannica International Ltd.)

The R.S.P.C.A. series (Diana Wyllie Ltd.)
In addition to transparencies, filmstrips and films are available direct from the R.S.P.C.A.

WALL PICTURES

Friends at the Zoo from *Friends Picture Set* by Frances Hook
God takes care of the Animals from *Present Day Pictures* by Frances Hook
Shepherds keeping watch from *Jesus Picture Set* by Frances Hook
David the Shepherd Boy from *Bible Picture Set* by Frances Hook
Shepherd Life from *Pictures of Life in Bible Times* by Wilbur Adam
  The above Picture Sets are available from the National Christian Education Council.

REFERENCE BOOKS

Man and Animals by R. E. Brett and Robert Broomfield (Hamish Hamilton)
British Wild Life by David Smith and Derek Newton (Blackie)
The Land where Jesus lived, Book 5, by E. R. Boyce (Macmillan)
The People and Lands of the Bible by R. W. Thomson (Hulton)
The Bible Reader's Encyclopaedia and Concordance (Collins)
Jungle
Tiger } *MacDonald Starter* (MacDonald Educational)
Elephants
Look at African Wildlife by Colin Willock (Hamish Hamilton)
Some strange animals by Paul Francois (George Harrap)
Nature Books for children – Second series by Edna Johnson (Basil Blackwell)
Animals Everywhere by Vera Croxford (Paul Hamlyn)
Wild Animals and their young by Jane Carruth (Odhams)
All about Squirrels and Moles and things by Althea and published for the National Trust by Dinosaur Publications Ltd.
Literature from The Wildlife Panda Club.

5. Colour

Starting Point

The colour of the children's clothes will provide plenty of discussion to commence this section. They can then be shown various pieces of coloured material which will involve them in further talking about their favourite colours.

Language Development

The children will talk freely about their favourite colours, and from thinking about the colours which they wear, enjoy through their toys, and in the painting and model making they can be encouraged to look further, and consider the colours in the world of nature. Look for colours in town and countryside.

SUGGESTIONS FOR CREATIVE WRITING

What is Red?
What is Green?
My Visit to the Land of Rainbows

The children can draw and colour a simple pattern. When this is done discuss with the children the meaning of the different colours, e.g. Green could be hidden emeralds; yellow could be a desert, blue could be a lake and orange could be a garden of magic flowers.

To get to the emeralds the children have to cross a lake and a desert. Also, they have to pass through the Magic Garden. They write about their adventures as they pass from colour to colour. This method of story telling can be effectively used in a Drama session. The children will have plenty of ideas as to what their colours represent.

STORIES TO BE READ OR TOLD

'The Story of a Rainbow' from *Stories for all Seasons* (National Christian Education Council)
'The Big Black Box' by Pauline M. Webb from *All God's Children* (Oliphants)
Up, Down and All Around by S. P. Russell (Concordia)
What Colour is Love by Joan Walsh Anglund (Collins)

What is Blue? by Mary O'Neill from *Bits and Pieces – poems for young readers* chosen by Peggy Blakeley (A. & C. Black)
Silver by Walter de la Mare from *First Poems, Book 3* (Schofield & Sims)

The Paint Box by E. V. Rieu ⎫ From *The Patchwork*
The Patchwork Quilt by Joan E. Cass ⎪ *Quilt and Other Poems*
White Fields by James Stephens ⎬ selected by Joan Cass
What is White by Mary O'Neill ⎭ (Longmans)

Art and Craft

The children can paint a 'beautiful' picture using not more than four colours. The pictures can be talked about, a title given to each one, and then a display mounted in the hall or corridor. 'Playplax' models can be built after which the children can talk about how the colours change when the sheets are placed close to each other.

Rainbow pictures can be made from Fabricrayons (Finart) and set alongside the hymn entitled 'Rainbow'. Overlay pictures can also be made using a variety of mediums. Older children can carry out Tie Dyeing.

Science

Let the children mix paints and learn from their experiments. The chart *How to Mix Colours* is very helpful and can be obtained from George Rowney & Co. Ltd.

Social Studies

It will be good to view paintings by great artists. There may be a selection in your school, or failing this a list of available postcard reproductions, transparencies and prints can be obtained from the National Gallery, the Tate Gallery and Athena Reproductions Ltd. Suggestions are made in the Further Source Material section. Personal transparencies of sunsets, sea scenes, and various aspects of nature will be useful.

Music

Talk with the children about colours being suggested by

music. Excerpts from well-known music can be played, e.g.
Piano Concerto in A Minor (Grieg) ASD 272
Morning from Peer Gynt (Grieg) MFP 2097
The Can-Can from La Boutique Fantasque (Rossini-Respighi) SXLP 30046
Finlandia Opus 26 (Sibelius) 7ER 5029

Religious Education
Develop a sense of appreciation for beautiful colours, and thankfulness for the fact that colour makes life interesting. Colours provide happiness and pleasure. Talk with the children about the colours that would have been seen around Lake Galilee when Jesus was there. The sea, fishing-boats, fishermen's clothes, the surrounding hills, the houses and the fish market at Capernaum.

BIBLICAL MATERIAL
The lilies of the field (Matthew 6: 28–29)
God's Promise in the rainbow (Genesis 9: 12–17)
Many precious stones are mentioned in the Bible. Reference to these can be found in a variety of Bible Encyclopaedias and Concordances.
Read Genesis Chapter 1 from *The Bible Story* by Philip Turner and Brian Wildsmith (O.U.P.)
Lydia, the dealer in purple cloth (Acts 16: 14).

PRAYERS: Throughout this section the wonder of God's handiwork will be developed, and the children will participate in producing their own contributions of colour and beauty. Prayers of thanks can be spoken spontaneously, and some can be written and integrated with Art and Craft work and the Social Studies when great artists' work will be appreciated.
Here is a responsive prayer which can be used in the classroom or during an Assembly:
For the blue sky and golden sun
Thank You, Father God
For the green grass and gay coloured flowers
Thank You, Father God

For the black roads and (red) buses
> *Thank You, Father God*

For bright clothes, beautiful jewels,
And the wonder of nature
> *Thank You, Father God*

HYMNS

All things bright and beautiful
The sun shines down on a beautiful world
For the beauty of the earth
Over the earth is a mat of green
Rainbow (From *New Child Songs* – Denholm House Press)

ASSEMBLY: This section can be brought to a close with A Festival of Beauty *or* Nature's Paint Box.

Further Source Material

TRANSPARENCIES   Sunsets, sea scenes and the countryside.
The Fighting Temeraire by Turner (National Gallery)
Vase of Flowers and Two Apples by Cézanne (National Gallery)

FILMSTRIP (for older children) *Let there be Light – Let there be Colour* (Concordia Films)

PRINTS

Donald Duck ⎫ These are both in bright colours and will
Magic Roundabout ⎬ attract the younger children. Available
⎭ from Athena Reproductions Ltd.

CHART
How to Mix Colours – George Rowney & Co. Ltd.

REFERENCE BOOKS
Colour – MacDonald Starter (MacDonald Educational)
All Things Bright and Beautiful – Glow-Worm series (E. J. Arnold)
Colours by Peggy Blakeley (A. & C. Black)
The Bible Story by Philip Turner and Brian Wildsmith (O.U.P.)
The Bible Reader's Encyclopaedia and Concordance (Collins)

ALL ABOUT ME

1. All About Me

This theme will need to be started in a general way before being broken down into the sections on the five senses. In this way the children will be encouraged to see themselves as whole persons with their senses being important in helping them to live contented and caring lives.

Starting Point
The children will talk readily about a variety of different aspects of themselves. They will talk about their likes and dislikes, and it is for each individual teacher to select the way in which the theme should develop. The children can be guided into talking about such things as 'What they are like to look at' 'Are they all the same?' 'What are the differences in each other?' Let them listen to the different sounds of their voices. What do they like to eat and drink? Why do they like the things they name?

Language Development
There will be many opportunities for conversation during the Starting Point.

SUGGESTIONS FOR WRITTEN WORK
Who am I?
I am a boy / girl whose name is ...... I live at ...... and I like ...... (the children can complete this alternative method of writing a description of themselves).
All About Me
My Favourite Things

STORIES TO BE READ OR TOLD
Joseph's Yard by Charles Keeping (O.U.P.)
A Dog so small by Phillipa Pearce (Puffin)
The Seven Stories of Robert Andrew series by Leonard Clark (E. J. Arnold)
Just Me by Marie Hall Ets (Angus and Robertson) (There is a filmstrip of this story available from Weston Woods Studios Ltd.)

Boy Jesus } by Wendy and Robert Wilkin
Boy David } (Denholm House Press)
Various stories from *Jesus Said* ...... by Beryl Bye and
Joyce Badrocke (Church Pastoral Aid Society)

POETRY

Every Time I Climb a Tree by David McCord } From *The Gol-*
I meant to do my work today by Richard le } *den Treasury*
Gallienne } *of Poetry*
selected and with a commentary by Louis Untermeyer
(Collins)
If I were an Apple – Poet unknown; from *Happy Landings* –
poems for the youngest chosen by Howard Sergeant (Evans)
I Remember by Thomas Hood from *The Swinging Rainbow* –
poems for the young selected by Howard Sergeant (Evans)
My Shadow by R. L. Stevenson from *A Child's Garden of Verse*
(Collins)
Reflections by Myra Cohn Livingston from *More Poems to read*
to the very young selected by Josette Frank (Odhams)

Art and Craft

An exhibition of photographs of the children from babyhood
onwards will show the children how they change and grow.

Draw round a boy and a girl. A group of children can then
dress the lifesize portraits in material from the scrap box.
The portraits can then be placed on a large wall panel ready
for labelling the five senses as the theme proceeds into the
breakdown of the separate sections. A display of items which
the children have made, pictures which have been painted;
in fact, anything which has been worked by the children at
school, home, church, Cub Scouts or Brownies can be
brought and exhibited. This will provide a link with the
development of the senses.

Mathematics

The children can work in pairs weighing and measuring each
other. Differences can be recorded. Footprints, handspans
and other body measurements can be compared and discussed. To emphasize the differences in height of a cross
section of the class at least six children can be measured

against a section of the wall and their heights marked off, and shown in centimetres.

Graphs of favourite television programmes; going to bed and getting up times, the colours of their hair and eyes, will add interest to the development of the whole theme.

Social Studies
The learning to be derived from such a theme as this is invaluable, but it is also important to help the children understand the importance of caring for others less fortunate than themselves. If it is possible help the children to respond to a 'need' within their community, and about which the children may have some knowledge.

The children can also be introduced to children in other lands. Oxfam can supply folders suitable for use with 7–9 year old children as follows:

Inti of Bolivia
Yanni of Greece
Gopal of India
Kim of Korea
Ali of Gaza

Music
My Favourite Things from *The Sound of Music*, RB 6616

P.E. and Movement
The children can test the agility and strength of their own bodies through various games skills, e.g. ball throwing and catching, work with bean bags, hoops and rings. Other skills such as balancing, jumping, stretching and curling can also be included.

Religious Education
In ancient times the name of a god or a person was supposed to reveal the character of the person. Therefore, names were very important, and this was so in Biblical times. Examples of the meaning of names: Abraham – father of a multitude; Moses – saved from water; David – beloved; Peter – rock or stone.

It would be interesting for the children to find out, or be told, the meaning of their own names.

BIBLICAL MATERIAL
If God cares for the sparrows he certainly cares for us! (Matthew 10: 29)
Jesus loves children (Mark 10: 13–16)
God made man (Genesis 1: 27 and Psalm 8: 3–6)

PRAYERS: *Inward Happiness*
Dear Father God, sometimes the blackbird hops to the topmost branch of a tree, and sings and sings as if something deep inside him makes him want to tell good news to everyone.
I can feel like that, too. Thank You, God, for Your Spirit of gladness everywhere.

from *Praying With Primaries* by Dorothy R. Wilton
(National Christian Education Council)
Other prayers in Section six of the above named book will also be helpful as will be those in the 'thinking' and 'thanking' sections of *Please God* by Beryl Bye and Joyce Badrocke (Church Pastoral Aid Society).

HYMNS
He Made Me
Life is a hymn for children ⎫ From *A Hymn for Children*
Always find time to pray ⎭ (High-Fye Music Ltd.)
For all the strength we have
Hands to work and feet to run
I'm very glad of God
When we are happy, full of fun ⎫ From *New Child Songs*
Clap, clap, clap, clap ⎬ (Denholm House Press)
When Jesus was a little boy ⎭

ASSEMBLY
All About Me
God cares for Me

Further Source Material
FILMSTRIP
Our Five Senses (selected frames) – (National Christian Education Council)

Getting to know God through His World (selected frames suitable for the older children) (Concordia Films)

WALL PICTURES

Conversation Pictures (*Through the Rainbow*) (Schofield & Sims)

Various pictures from the Frances Hook series (from National Christian Education Council)

BOOKS

My First Book of Thanks – Glow-Worm series (E. J. Arnold)

Round and Round by Althea (Souvenir Press Ltd.)

A variety of leaflets and papers listing sources of information regarding personal hygiene, and good health are available from the Health Education Council.

The Bible Reader's Encyclopaedia and Concordance (Collins)

2. Seeing

The general approach to the theme of 'All About Me' can stand by itself or provide a basis for proceeding to the sections: Seeing, Hearing, Touch, Smell and Taste.

Starting Point
Selected frames from the filmstrip *Our Five Senses* can be used to introduce each section. Also, a special 'table' or 'corner' can be established to focus continued attention on the section. A Sight Table can be set up containing colourful objects, and pictures with objects hidden in them. A Wall Panel close to the Sight Table can be used to display visual aids about blind people learning various skills such as Braille. Pictures of a blind person and a guide dog can also be shown as they train together.

Language Development
Play the game 'I Spy'. Place some new items at strategic places in the room. Have they been noticed by the children? Develop their sense of seeing and observing by asking the children to notice details about the objects, then remove them and let the children describe the objects.

Suggestions for Written Work
Draw and write about the missing objects.
Things I like to see
The day I pretended to be blind
Take the children to the playground, or another suitable place to observe what is happening there. They can then make a list of the things that they have not before noticed.

Stories to be read or told
The Beggar's Greatest Wish – Arch Book (Concordia)
Dancing in the Dark by Pauline M. Webb from *All God's Children* (Oliphants)
I open my eyes – Glow-Worm series (E. J. Arnold)
A simplified story about Louis Braille

63

POETRY

Reflection by Myra Cohn Livingston from *More Poems to read to the very young* selected by Josette Frank (Odhams)

Joys by J. R. Lowell ⎫ From *Come Follow Me –*
Shining Things by Elizabeth Gould ⎬ *poems for the very young*
In the Mirror by Elizabeth Fleming ⎭ (Evans)

Art and Craft

Label the eyes of the models made for the general approach to the theme. The appropriate verse from the hymn 'He made Me' can be written out and placed close to the models.

The children can work individually, or in groups to paint scenes, make collages or clay models of things recently seen.

Social Studies

Show the children examples of Braille, and emphasize the fact that we can see the wonders of the world all around us, but that people who are blind cannot see the beauty that we take for granted. Material can be obtained from the Guide Dogs for the Blind Association, and the Royal National Institute for the Blind.

In some countries such as India children and grown-ups have eye diseases which cannot be cured and they become blind. Encourage the children to save aluminium foil which can be their contribution towards helping to purchase a guide dog.

Religious Education

BIBLICAL MATERIAL

The Story of Blind Bartimaeus (Mark 10: 46–52)
Jesus met a man who had been blind since birth (John 9: 1)
Peter, one of Jesus' friends, tells people about the things he saw Him do when He was alive (Acts 10: 36–39a)

PRAYERS: Have a colourful vase of flowers on display, and say a prayer of thanks with the children whilst everyone is looking at the flowers.

Father God, help me to keep my eyes wide open, and to see all the beautiful things in your world. Amen.

Lord, we have the wonderful gift of sight, but there are

people who are blind. Please help the people who work
    to train guide dogs
    in the St. Dunstan's organization
    for the Royal National Institute for the Blind
    in the Helen Keller Home
(select one of these that the children have heard about
through the Social Studies)
and help us to remember the kindness of these people. Amen.

The children can compose their own prayers about things
which they have seen and come to appreciate as this section
has been developed.

HYMNS

He made Me (relevant verses) from *A Hymn for Children* (High
Fye Music Ltd.)
I love to think that Jesus saw (From *New Child Songs*, Denholm
House Press)
Teach me, my God and King

ASSEMBLY

All things bright and beautiful
God gave us eyes to see the wonders of His world

Further Source Material

FILMSTRIP

Our Five Senses (National Christian Education Council)

WALL PICTURES

God gives me beautiful things from *Present Day Picture Set* by
Frances Hook (from National Christian Education Council)
Other pictures of colourful and beautiful items

REFERENCE BOOKS

Look at your eyes by Paul Showers (A. & C. Black)
We Discover Light, Lenses and Colour by R. H. C. Fice & I. M.
Simkiss (E. J. Arnold)
Blue Peter Book of Guide Dogs (B.B.C.)
Guide Dogs for the Blind by Dorothy Clewes (Guide Dogs for
the Blind Association)
Leaflets giving background information about blindness,
especially the work of the Sunshine Homes is available from

the Royal National Institute for the Blind. The training of guide dogs, and how the blind learn to use them, is set out in pamphlets available from the Guide Dogs for the Blind Association. A pack of illustrated literature, and a set of six wall charts are available from St. Dunstan's.

FILM (*for Staff*): 16mm. Black and White *I Have an Egg*. This is a Polish film about the discovery, by a blind child, of the shape and texture of an egg. Available from Concord Films Council.

3. Hearing

Starting Point

The relevant frames of *Our Five Senses* can be viewed or shown later as the section unfolds thus providing reinforcement to learning already encountered by the children. As an alternative the children can take turns in speaking their names and listening to the sounds produced. They can also clap their hands to various rhythms. A 'hearing' table can be established. There should be a selection of musical instruments available so that children can produce their own sounds. Pictures of objects which provide everyday sounds should be available, e.g. aeroplanes, cars, and items relevant to the school environment. Psalm 150 can be written out and placed close to the musical instruments.

Language Development

Clearness of speech is very important for both the teacher and the children. Correct pronunciation can be emphasized by letting the children use a toy telephone for conversation across the classroom. Word building and similar sounding words with different spellings can be developed through this section. This will be beneficial to individual children.

SUGGESTIONS FOR WRITTEN WORK: The children can list the following types of sound which they can hear on most days. The teacher will be able to select those which are suitable for the local situation:

Soft and loud sounds
Happy and unpleasant sounds
Hurrying sounds (e.g. ambulance, fire engine)
Sounds of the city; the sea and the countryside

The children can write their own story about sounds which they would like to hear.

STORIES TO BE READ OR TOLD
How the Nightingale got its Voice – Glow-Worm series (E. J. Arnold)
This is God's World–Listen! – Glow-Worm series (E. J. Arnold)

A simply told story about Helen Keller

POETRY

Laughing Song by William Blake from *Poetry Panorama, Book 2* (Odhams)

The Rain by W. H. Davies from *Poetry Panorama, Book 1* (Odhams)

The Shell – part of a poem by James Stephens from *Bits and Pieces – poems for young readers* chosen by Peggy Blakeley (A. & C. Black)

Art and Craft

Label the ears of the models made for the general approach to the theme. Incorporate the relevant verse of He Made Me from A Hymn for Children (High-Fye Music Ltd.). What colours are suggested by sounds and music? The children can listen to various extracts from pop and classical music (see the Music section). As they listen they can paint, or wax crayon shapes, according to what the music suggests to them. When the art work is finished talk about the shapes and colours with the children.

Toy telephones can be made. The children will need two empty tins with holes already punched, and the metal smoothed down, in the bottom of each tin, a long piece of string and some wax. Wax the string and then thread the ends through the holes making sure that secure knots are tied on the inside. When this is done two children can go into the playground or separate corners of the room with their 'telephone'. One child holds a tin to his ear whilst the other speaks into the second tin. What can be heard? What happens when the string is slack? What happens when it is taut?

Music and Sounds

The following recordings will be useful

Children EFX 116

Weather effects / Country Sounds EFX 109

City Traffic and Transport EFX 112

Seaside EFX 108

There are other records available in this series from E.M.I. Records, Hayes, Middlesex. Contrast the clear diction of the singing of *I Know that My Redeemer Liveth* (HQS 1183) with the way in which a current pop song is communicated.

Ask the children to bring their own favourite records, but try to maintain a balance between the pop scene, and light classical music. It may be helpful to supplement the collection with records from the School Record Library.

What are the children's thoughts as they listen to the following

Nun's Chorus from Casanova (J. Strauss) sung by June Bronhill SCX 6359

Sprach Zarathrustra Bronhill SCX 6359

Pomp and Circumstance March No. 1 in D Minor (Elgar) SDD 255

Conclusion to the 3rd Movement of the Piano Concerto in A Minor (Grieg) ASD 272

Music can also be composed by the children on glockenspiels and other instruments available in the school.

Develop accompaniment with percussion instruments for the hymn 'For all the strength we have,' and the poem *Forest Pools* by Leonard Clark from *Drums and Trumpets* (Bodley Head)

Religious Education

BIBLICAL MATERIAL

Many of the musical instruments of the bible are mentioned in Psalm 150

When David was a young man he played the harp to comfort King Saul (I Samuel 16: 23)

Various writers of the psalms tell us to sing and make a joyful noise to God (Psalms 95: 1, 96: 1, 98: 1, 4–5)

If you have ears for hearing, listen. Listen to what you hear (Mark 4: 23–24)

PRAYERS: Father God, I can hear many sounds. There are traffic sounds, aeroplane sounds, musical sounds (let the children supply their own list). Deaf people cannot hear these sounds, but please help them to enjoy seeing beautiful things in Your world. Amen.

After the children have listened to a piece of music or composed their own piece on an instrument they can write prayers of thanks for pleasant sounds.

Use the prayer entitled 'Minds' from *Praying With Primaries* by Dorothy R. Wilton (National Christian Education Council).

HYMNS

Stamp and Shout from *New Songs for the Church* (Galliard)

Sing a glad song from *The Morning Cockerel Hymnbook* (Rupert Hart-Davis)

Clap, clap, clap
Let's be quiet
Let's beat a song of praise
(to be used with percussion) } From *New Child Songs* (Denholm House Press)

ASSEMBLY

Make a joyful noise to God!

Let's be happy and sing!

Thank You, God, for the wonder of hearing

Further Source Material

FILMSTRIP

Our Five Senses (National Christian Education Council)

WALL PICTURES

Three girls singing from *Present Day Picture Set*
David the Shepherd from *Bible Picture Set* } by Frances Hook (from National Christian Education Council)

REFERENCE BOOKS

The Sounds of the City
The Sounds of the Sea
The Sounds of the Country } by W. Bulman (Rupert Hart-Davis)

We Discover Sounds and Music by R. H. C. Fice and I. M. Simkiss (E. J. Arnold)

The Listening Walk
How You Talk } by Paul Showers (A. & C. Black)

This is God's World – Listen! Glow Worm series (E. J. Arnold)

The Bible Reader's Encyclopaedia & Concordance (Collins)

The People and Lands of the Bible by R. W. Thomson (Hulton)

Things I Like series – Sounds by Peggy Blakeley (A. & C. Black)

4. Touch

Starting Point
This section can be started with the relevant frames of the filmstrip *Our Five Senses*. As an alternative a number of objects can be produced and passed around amongst groups of children. Find a selection with various textures, e.g. sandpaper, fur, velvet, silk, damp sponge, marble, dog biscuit and a number of metal objects to link with the Science activity. When the children have handled the items they can be removed and the children asked to name, or list, as many as possible. The items can then be used to start the display on the Touch Table.

Language Development
This will already have been started in the Starting Point but it can be extended into using special words to describe the objects. This can be continued with the questions, 'Which . . . tall or short?' Which other objects feel rough? 'Which objects are round, smooth, large, small, tall or short?'

SUGGESTIONS FOR WRITTEN WORK
After a visit to the Touch Table children can write about the objects.
Things I like to touch
My Teddy feels soft and cuddly (the children can finish a short story started by the teacher)
My kitten
The day that everything turned liquid / sticky / plastic / foamy / slippery

STORIES TO BE READ OR TOLD
The Little Sleeping Beauty – Arch Book (Concordia)
Velvet the Kitten by Anne-Marie Pajet (Nelson)

POETRY
Woolly Blanket by Kate Cox Goddard from *More Poems to read to the very young* selected by Josette Frank (Odhams)
The Black Pebble by James Reeves from *The Patchwork Quilt and Other Poems* selected by Joan Cass (Longmans)

Art and Craft

Label the hands and feet of the models made for the general approach to the theme, and incorporate the relevant verse from 'He Made Me' to be found in *A Hymn for Children* (High-Fye Music Ltd.)

A collage or wall chart can be made using various rough and smooth textured materials.

Science

Experiments with magnets can be carried out on the objects placed on the Touch table. Which objects are picked up? Which are left behind? What type of object is picked up?

Religious Education

BIBLICAL MATERIAL

Jesus liked to have children near Him. He would put His arms around them (Mark 10: 16)

They brought children for Him to touch (Mark 10: 13, New English Bible)

Some of the clothes worn in the days of Jesus were very rough. John the Baptist wore rough clothes which were made from camel's hair (Mark 1: 6)

PRAYERS: Talk with the children about the kind and gentle hands of the people who help them when they are unwell, e.g. parents, doctors, nurses, dentists. Prayers can then be written to develop this aspect of the section.

Dear God, every day I use my hands all the time:
    to dress with,
    to eat with,
    to paint and write with,
    to carry things . . .
      (Children may suggest other ways).

Thank You, God, for strong and busy hands. Amen
(from *Praying With Primaries* by Dorothy R. Wilton – National Christian Education Council)

HYMNS

Jesus' hands were kind hands

The kitten's fur is warm (from *New Child Songs* – Denholm House Press)

It fell upon a summer day from *School Assembly Hymnbook* (Denholm House Press)

Further Source Material

FILMSTRIP

Our Five Senses (National Christian Education Council)

WALL PICTURES

The School Dentist
A Friendly Nurse } From *Friends Picture Set* by Frances Hook

My Daddy Loves Me ⎱ From *Present Day Picture Set* by
Now I lay me down to sleep ⎰ Frances Hook

Homemade clothing from *Pictures of Life in Bible Times* by Wilbur Adam

The above picture sets are available from the National Christian Education Council

REFERENCE BOOKS

My Hands ⎱
Find out by Touching ⎰ by Paul Showers (A. & C. Black)

The Land Where Jesus Lived, Book 3, by E. R. Boyce (Macmillan)

The People and Lands of the Bible by R. W. Thomson (Hulton)

Things I Like series – Rough and Smooth by Peggy Blakeley (A. & C. Black)

Useful samples of materials can be obtained from the following: The Flaxspinners' & Manufacturers' Association of Great Britain, 4, Chamber of Commerce Buildings, Dundee, Scotland. Silk Education Centre, 10 Cliffe Road, Barton-on-Sea, Hants.

5. Smell

Starting Point

By working in groups the children can enjoy some of the scents and smells of every day life, e.g. a bowl of fruit, a vase of flowers. Then progress to a 'smelling' game based on the idea of Kim's Game. The technique of Kim's Game is to exercise the memory. It is usually played in groups who view various objects. These are then removed from sight and the players list orally or in writing as many as possible of the objects which they have viewed. Use items such as cheese, coffee, oranges, lavender and so on. The children can be trusted to keep their eyes closed whilst the group game is in progress! To continue the aspect of displaying items relevant to each of the five senses a Table can be set-up on which various items can be displayed.

Language Development

Talk to the children about various smells such as the smell of the kitchen at home, the School Dining Hall, favourite food (fish and chips, strawberry jelly, sausages and beans), the garden, the street, the seaside. The children will also add their own suggestions.

SUGGESTIONS FOR WRITTEN WORK: My Favourite Smells. Lists of pleasant and unpleasant smells can be made on the blackboard and discussed, e.g. the unpleasant smell of diesel fumes from buses and lorries; the pleasant smell of freshly mown grass, of bacon and eggs, and a roast dinner.

Art and Craft

The relevant label can be added to the models of the children. Perhaps teachers and children can work together to compose a verse to place alongside those already by the model, and which were selected from the hymn 'He Made Me'.

Paintings and Wax Crayon pictures can be made of Mummy cooking the dinner, and of the suggestions made when the children talked about pleasant and unpleasant smells.

Social Studies
The value and importance of fresh air can be stressed. This is a part of our world which is being spoiled by smoke and fuels.

Religious Education
PRAYERS: The children can write their own prayers of thanks according to the pictures which they will make. The prayers can then be attached to the art work.

HYMNS
For the beauty of the earth (relevant verses)
Clap, clap, clap (verse 2) from *New Child Songs* (Denholm House Press)

Further Source Materials
FILMSTRIP
Our Five Senses (National Christian Education Council)

REFERENCE BOOKS
Follow Your Nose by Paul Showers (A. & C. Black)
Smells I Like – Glow-Worm series (E. J. Arnold)

6. Taste

Starting Point

When the children become involved in this section with the taste of various foods there is likely to be an integration with the section on 'Smell'. This will be good as the children will be learning about the properties of food, and not separating items into purely taste, or smell. Our senses work together for our pleasure and enjoyment.

Give each child a piece of apple or orange. Do they like the taste? What other tastes do they like?

A table of 'Tastes' can be set up containing salt, sugar, a lemon, melon, ginger, vinegar, a piece of chocolate. Try to arrange for the children to taste items as they work in their groups.

Language Development

SUGGESTIONS FOR WRITTEN WORK

The Land of Lovely Tastes

The Day I put the tastes in the ice cream (or any other food that the children choose)

STORY TO BE READ OR TOLD

Salt by Harve and Margot Zemach (Faber). There is also a filmstrip available from Weston Woods Studios Ltd.

POETRY

If I were an apple – poet unknown; from *Happy Landings – poems for the youngest* chosen by Howard Sergeant (Evans)

This is just to say by William Carlos Williams from *Bits and Pieces – poems for young readers* chosen by Peggy Blakeley (A. & C. Black)

Blackberries by John Walsh from *Bits and Pieces* (A. & C. Black)

Goblin Market by Christina Rossetti from *Come Follow Me – poems for the very young* (Evans)

Art and Craft

Label the model children to show taste. Also, the children

and teacher can work together to produce a suitable verse about taste to be placed with the other verses now attached close to the models.

The children can work in groups to make a collage to illustrate the 'Land of Lovely Tastes'. Individual paintings can also accompany the written work about putting the taste in the ice-cream.

Science

What are sugar, salt and various spices used for in cooking? Educational material distributed by the British Sugar Bureau can be obtained from Educational Productions Ltd., East Ardsley, Wakefield, Yorks. An experiment separating the salt from salt water can be carried out. Let the children taste the residue.

Social Studies

Where does sugar come from? The children can be introduced to work about the West Indies. Samples of the various sugars can be on display. Large posters are available from Government and Tourist Offices.

Also, work can be carried out on other foods such as various spices, lemons, melons, ginger, chocolate, coffee and cheese. Material for the two latter named items can be obtained from the following sources:

The Coffee Promotion Council Ltd., BBDO Public Relations Ltd., Berk House, 8 Baker Street, London, W.1.

The Cheese Bureau, 40 Berkeley Square, London W1X 6AD
The Dutch Dairy Bureau, The Dutch House, 307/8 High Holborn, London WC1V 7LP

Religious Education

BIBLICAL MATERIAL

The palate (or tongue) tastes food (Job 12: 11)
Honey tastes sweet to the tongue (Psalm 119: 103)

PRAYERS: Have a bowl of fruit as a focal point and use the prayer *Our Senses* from *Praying With Juniors* by Jack and Edna Young (National Christian Education Council)

After using this prayer the children can speak or write

their own prayers for other tastes which they enjoy. Smell, colour and shape can be incorporated into written work.

HYMNS

See here are red apples (From *Nursery Song and Picture Book*, Religious Education Press)

What makes the daytime (verse 4)
Ears of corn are listening (verses 2 and 3)
} From *New Child Songs* (Denholm House Press)

ASSEMBLY

Our Favourite Tastes

Further Source Material

FILMSTRIPS

Our Five Senses (National Christian Education Council)
Salt (Weston Woods Studios Ltd.)

WALL PICTURES

The boy saying grace
The boy with his basket of strawberries
} From *Present Day Picture Set* by Frances Hook (from National Christian Education Council)

REFERENCE BOOKS

Teeth
Apples
} MacDonald Starters (MacDonald Educational)
How many teeth by Paul Showers (A. & C. Black)
Let's Visit the West Indies (Burke)
Sugar
Salt
Cocoa and Chocolate
} by O. B. Gregory (Wheaton)
Salt by Augusta Goldin (A. & C. Black)

THEME FOUR

FOOD

1. Bread
2. Fish
3. Fruit
4. Parties
5. Harvest

1. Bread

Starting Point
It will be good to have a selection of loaves on display, e.g.
Coburg, granary, Vienna, cottage, croissants, and a long
French loaf. The children can choose which they would like
to taste, and in groups they could have a piece of bread and
butter. Alternatives to this activity are
    (*a*) A visit to a Bakery or,
    (*b*) A visit to a farm to see the machinery used to gather
in the harvest of the fields.

Language Development
Discuss with the children the importance of bread. How
many times a day do we eat bread? It is a part of our staple
diet. Tell the children how Father used to be known as the
breadwinner.

SUGGESTIONS FOR WRITTEN WORK: If the children have
been out on a visit they can present a written report as well
as talk about it with their teacher.

CREATIVE WRITING
I am a mouse in a cornfield
My Work in a Bakery
The day I was in charge of the Combine Harvester

STORIES TO BE READ OR TOLD
'The boy who shared his lunch' – Arch Book (Concordia)
'An African Harvest Festival' } From *Stories for all Seasons*
'Mutesa's Adventure' } (National Christian
Education Council)
'The King and His Son' from *Rainbows End* (Schofield &
Sims)

POETRY
Bread by H. E. Wilkinson } From *Come Follow Me –*
Harvest Home – poet unknown } *poems for the very young* (Evans)

Art and Craft
A model of a Baker's Shop can be made from large cardboard

boxes and pieces of card. Bread wrappers and pictures of bread can be mounted on card and used along with the shop for Mathematics. Individual large pictures of loaves can be made, and the ingredients written around the perimeter of the picture. Plastic Meccano and wooden building materials can be used for making Combine Harvesters. Grinding stones such as those used in Palestine can be made from clay. Paintings of modern day scenes in the fields when the corn is gathered can be contrasted with paintings of harvest time in the fields when Jesus and His disciples walked through them.

Science
The children can bake some bread. There are many easy recipes and this should be a worthwhile activity for the children to do in small groups. Grow some barley in a transparent container. This can be done in the same way as growing beans, or the barley can be sown in a bowl. Let the children watch the growth. The Flour Advisory Bureau will supply material including samples from the various stages of flour milling.

Mathematics
Practical mathematics will occur when the children weigh the ingredients for the bread. Work with money, involving practical work and some computation, will develop from purchasing the ingredients from the Baker's Shop made in an Art and Craft session.

Social Studies
Introduce the children to the fact that some children in other countries have a different kind of food as a part of their staple diet, e.g. yams in the West Indies, and rice in India and Hong Kong.

P.E. and Movement
The children can work in small groups in movements depicting wheat waving in the wind. The Combine Harvesters then set to work cutting the wheat, sorting and baling it ready to be transported from the farm.

Religious Education

Jesus always remembered to thank God for food at mealtimes (John 6: 23)

The five barley loaves and two fishes (John 6: 5–13)

Joseph gives the people corn seed (Genesis 47: 23–24)

Jeremiah was given a daily ration of one loaf (Jeremiah 37: 21) (emphasizing the importance of bread as a part of one's diet)

The valleys are thick with corn (Psalm 65: 13)

Ruth gleaned in the fields, and collected about an ephah (bushel) of barley (Ruth 2: 17)

PRAYERS:

Give us this day our daily bread. This section of the Lord's Prayer is explained in *The Lord's Prayer* by Mary Alice Jones (Collins).

Give us today the food we need (Matthew 6: 11 from *Good News for Modern Man* – Collins).

The children can speak and write their own prayers for the bread which they enjoy. If this section is used at Harvest time the children can compose prayers of thanks for the farmers who work hard to produce the corn, so that we have bread to eat. God's care through the rain and the sunshine for producing good crops should also be emphasized.

HYMNS

Father, bless our bread and meat (From *The Morning Cockerel Hymnbook* – Rupert Hart-Davis)

First the seed and then the grain (From *New Child Songs* – Denholm House Press)

Reapers in the cornfield (From *Sing a New Song* by Bridget Ball – Religious Education Press)

We thank you, O God, for your goodness (From *Faith, Folk and Clarity* – Galliard)

ASSEMBLY

Thank You, Father God, for our bread.

Further Source Material

WALL PICTURES

A Boy's Lunch ⎫ From the *Jesus Picture Set* by
He took bread and blessed it ⎭ Frances Hook

God gives me Food from the *Present Day Picture Set* by Frances Hook

Ruth from the *Bible Picture Set* by Frances Hook

Grinding and Baking ⎫
Sowing Seed ⎪ From the *Life in Bible Times Picture*
Winnowing ⎬ *Set* by Wilbur Adam
Ploughing ⎭

The above-mentioned Picture Sets are available from the National Christian Education Council.

Feeding the 5,000 – from *The Teaching of Christ Picture Set* (Nelson)

REFERENCE BOOKS

The Land where Jesus lived, Book 3, by E. R. Boyce (Macmillan)
People and Lands of the Bible by R. W. Thomson (Hulton)
Life in New Testament Times (Ladybird)
Bread – MacDonald Starter (MacDonald Educational)
Busy People by Lene Hille-Brandts and Doris Dumber (W. & R. Chambers)

2. Fish

Starting Point
If the school is situated within a reasonable distance of a fishing port a visit would set the scene well. Alternatively make a display of frozen fish packets, or exhibit briefly a piece of wet fish. The school aquarium may also be used to advantage.

Language Development
Factual reports, both verbal and written can be made on the visit. A news story about 'Our Aquarium' can also be useful in renewing interest in the fish that children see each day.

SUGGESTIONS FOR CREATIVE WRITING
What is a Fish?
My Fishing Trip
Some of the fish I met on my Underwater Adventure

STORIES TO BE READ OR TOLD
David goes Fishing by Elisabeth Beresford (Ernest Benn)
The Fishermen's Surprise – Arch Book (Concordia)
The Boy who shared his lunch – Arch Book (Concordia)

POETRY
Little Johnny from *Happy Landings – poems for the youngest* chosen by Howard Sergeant (Evans)
The Fishermen's Boats by Annie Wrench from *Passport to Poetry, Book 2* (Cassell)
The Boy Fishing by Edith Scovell from *Bits and Pieces – poems for young readers* chosen by Peggy Blakeley (A. & C. Black)

Art and Craft
Decorative fish can be made and used as mobiles. Some can be suspended in a model aquarium and others from suitable places in the room. A frieze of various types of fishing boat can be made from pictures collected from magazines and educational journals. A large fishing-boat can be made from soap boxes and other junk. Paintings of Jesus and the fishermen can also be made.

Pictures of Galilean fishing scenes, especially the fishing-boats will need to be collected. These can provide useful visual information and can be displayed on a wall panel.

Science
The children can work in groups to look after the school aquarium. Care will need to be exercised in feeding the fish and cleaning the aquarium.

Social Studies
Where does the fish we eat come from? Use the map *Where Britain's Fish is Caught*, available from White Fish Authority. Which fish are caught in the fishing grounds around our coasts. What kinds of fish did the friends of Jesus catch?

P.E. and Movement
Develop strong body movements such as pushing and pulling. Link this with the activity of pushing out the Galilean fishing-boats, and the casting of the fishing nets. Games can include Flapping the Fish and a Magnetic Fish Game.

Religious Education
BIBLICAL MATERIAL
Jesus and His friends who were fishermen (Mark 1: 16–20)
Jesus having breakfast on the beach with the fishermen (John 21: 9–13)
Tell the children about the famous fishing towns such as Capernaum.

PRAYERS: Our Father God, when we go to the sea we see the big ships sailing far out to sea. Sometimes we see the little fishing boats, and the fishermen who go out bravely to catch the fish while we are safely sleeping in our beds. Please take care of them, and sailors everywhere. (From *Praying With Primaries* by Dorothy R. Wilton – National Christian Education Council)
The children after hearing and reading such a prayer can then write their own prayers for fishermen.

HYMNS

The Fishermen ⎫ From *Sing a New Song* by Bridget Ball
Sea Song ⎭ (Religious Education Press)
Peter's Brown Boat (From *Nursery Song and Picture Book* –
Religious Education Press)
When lamps are lighted in the town (From *Infant Praise* –
O.U.P.)
Push out the boat, Peter (From *New Child Songs* – Denholm
House Press)

ASSEMBLY

Fish is good for us
Brave Men who catch our fish
Jesus and His Fishermen Friends

Further Source Material

WALL PICTURES

Fishermen from the Picture set *Life in Bible Times* by Wilbur
Adam (from National Christian Education Council)

Pictures of fishermen and their boats can be supplied by
some Local Authorities. Relevant pictures from *New World*
by Alan T. Dale (O.U.P.)

MAP

Where Britain's Fish is Caught (The White Fish Authority)

REFERENCE BOOKS

Fish by Brian Wildsmith (O.U.P.)
Fish – MacDonald Starter (MacDonald Educational)
We Discover an Aquarium by R. H. Fice and I. M. Simkiss
(E. J. Arnold)
Fish from the Sea by Dawn Lovitt (Basil Blackwell)
Fishermen by O. B. Gregory (Wheaton)
The Trawler Captain by M. Hyde (Macmillan)
The People and Lands of the Bible by R. W. Thomson (Hulton)
Life in Bible Times by Clifford M. Jones (Denholm House
Press)
Jesus by the Sea of Galilee ⎫
Jesus calls His disciples ⎪
The Story of Peter the Fisherman ⎬ (Ladybird)
The Fisherman ⎭

3. Fruit

Starting Point
A bowl of various kinds of fruit will soon start the children talking about their favourite fruit. This section could also be started with a visit, if possible, to a wholesale fruit merchant or a fruit farm or a market.

Language Development
After a discussion about the various kinds of fruit that will have been seen on a visit, or which is available in the fruit bowl, the children can learn how the fruit is obtained, e.g. apples may come from a tree in the garden, or the greengrocer who will have bought them from the wholesale fruit merchant. Where does he get them? How do they get there? Where were they grown? Other fruits such as oranges and bananas can be dealt with in the same way.

SUGGESTIONS FOR WRITTEN WORK
A report of a visit
My visit to the apple orchard
The Magic Banana

STORY TO BE READ OR TOLD
'The Story of Johnny Appleseed' from *Tell Me a Tale* by Elizabeth Clark (U.L.P.)

POETRY
Cherries – poet unknown; from *Passport to Poetry, Book 2*, by E. L. Black and D. S. Davies (Cassell)
This is just to say by William Carlos Williams from *Bits and Pieces – poems for young readers* chosen by Peggy Blakeley (A. & C. Black)
Goblin Market by Christina Rossetti from *Come Follow Me – poems for the very young* (Evans)
   Other suitable poems can be found in the 'Taste' section of the theme: 'All About Me'.

Art and Craft
Large wax crayon or Fabricrayon pictures of individual fruits will make a colourful display for a wall panel.

Groups can also make collages of Apple Orchards, Orange Groves and perhaps a scene of how the fruit is transported from the grower to the shops.

Science
Plant Avocado stones. Full instructions and interesting information is available from Centrehurst Ltd.

Mathematics
The shop which was made for the Bread section can be brought into use again, this time as a fruit market. The children can gain experience in work with money and weighing.

Social Studies
Talk with the children about the fruit they enjoy which comes from other countries, e.g. oranges from Israel, apples from New Zealand, bananas from the Canary Islands and the West Indies.

They can begin to develop an understanding of how we depend on people in other lands for many of the fruits, and other food, that we enjoy.

Religious Education
BIBLICAL MATERIAL
The grapevines which grew everywhere in the Holy Land (Matthew 20: 1–16; Isaiah 5: 1–7)
Olives and Olive Oil (Exodus 23: 11)
Figs (I Samuel 30: 12 (cake of figs); Luke 13: 6)

PRAYERS: The children should be ready to respond spontaneously with their thanks after enjoying some fruit. Perhaps this can be arranged, after which they speak or write their own prayers of thanks.

Prayers can also be written for the people who work to provide us with the fruit.

HYMNS

See here are red apples (From the *Nursery Song and Picture Book* – Religious Education Press)
Reapers in the Cornfields – verse 2 (From *Sing a New Song* by Bridget Ball – Religious Education Press)
All things bright and beautiful (relevant verse)
For all the strength we have

ASSEMBLY

Thank You, dear Lord, for the ripe fruits

Further Source Material

FILMSTRIP (for the older children)
Getting to know God through His World (selected frames) (Concordia Films)

TRANSPARENCY
Still Life with Apples – Cézanne (Tate Gallery Publications)

REFERENCE BOOKS
The People and Lands of the Bible by R. W. Thomson (Hulton)
Fruit and Vegetables – First Interest, Book 4 (Ginn & Co.)
Life in New Testament Times (Ladybird)

WALL PICTURES
The Boy with the strawberries (From the *Present Day Picture Set* by Frances Hook)
The Vineyard from the *Life in Bible Times Picture Set* by Wilbur Adam
The above Picture Sets are available from the National Christian Education Council.

4. Parties

Starting Point

Food is always an important part of any party. Talk about the favourite foods that children enjoy on such occasions. Have a Welcome Back Party at the beginning of a new term. This can be arranged in groups with the children eating sandwiches, crisps or biscuits with a drink of squash.

Language Development

The children can write a report of their Welcome Back Party.

SUGGESTIONS FOR CREATIVE WRITING

The Fantastic Tea Party

The Animals have a Party

An oral story can be started by the teacher and finished by the children.

STORIES TO BE READ OR TOLD

'The Birthday Party' from *All God's Children* by Pauline M. Webb (Oliphants)

'*Topsy and Tim's Friday Book*' by Jean and Gareth Adamson (Blackie)

'*The Midnight Party*' by Peggy Blakeley (A. & C. Black)

'The story of the three parties' from *Jesus Said . . .* by Beryl Bye and Joyce Badrocke (Church Pastoral Aid Society)

POETRY

Betty at the Party – poet unknown ⎫ From *Come Follow Me* –
The Pirate's Tea Party by Dorothy ⎬ *poems for the very young*
Una Ratcliffe ⎭ (Evans)

Art and Craft

The children can make a collage of 'Party Time'. This can include the preparation of the food, games and party clothes. A boy and a girl can be drawn round to produce life size models, and then dressed in fancy dress for a party.

Science

Talk about how the party food is made. Where does it come

from? How does it come to us? Cakes can be made for the remainder of the children in the Year Group. An easy cake mix can be prepared on arrival one morning. The children can then have a cake in the afternoon, and this activity can be linked with an Assembly.

Mathematics

Children can visit the school, or classroom shop to purchase the ingredients for cake making. Practical work in weighing the ingredients can take place, and some recording can be done. Block Graphs can be made showing the children's favourite Party Games.

Social Studies

The Wendy House or Home Corner can be used to encourage conversation in planning a party. Help the children to think about inviting those who are left out of games and other activities.

Music

Tijuana Nursery Rhymes MFP 1331
Whipped Cream Pye International 7N 25292
Songs for Singing Children SZ 218 (E. J. Arnold)
A Party Record 7 EG 128

Games

Group and Class Games can precede the food. These can include 'Oranges and Lemons', 'Pass the Parcel', various balloon games, and *Movement to Zorba's Dance* (Durium DRS 54001)

Religious Education

Give some thought to children who do not have parties. There are children at home and overseas who are lonely. Some are unhappy because of homelessness. Shelter will provide information on these children. Other children live in war torn and refugee areas. Save the Children and Christian Aid will supply information about these children. Think about the children who live in lands where there is a lack of food and water.

BIBLICAL MATERIAL
Jesus went to a wedding party (John 2: 1–2)

PRAYERS: Help the children to say their own prayers which can be used as a Grace before the party food. After the fun and games the children can write prayers of thanks, and prayers for those children who cannot go to parties.

HYMNS
All good gifts around us
Sing a glad song to Christ the King from *The Morning Cockerel* (Rupert Hart-Davis)
If the party is held after the Christmas holiday use 'Song of Christmas' from *Sing a New Song* by Bridget Ball (Religious Education Press)

ASSEMBLY
Let's Have a Party
We enjoy Parties
This can be a year group gathering. The children who enjoyed their own class party will have shared in making and distributing cakes to other children. The Assembly can be held in the afternoon just before going home.

Further Source Material
WALL PICTURES

Thank You, God from the *Present Day Picture Set*	by Frances Hook (from National Christian Education Council)
Friends from Everywhere from the *Friends Picture Set*	

5. Harvest

Work for Harvest time can be readily evolved from any one of the sections within this theme, and the section entitled 'Water' in the Creation theme. It may well be that teachers will wish to include more than one aspect of the food we eat, and in this case material can be selected from a cross section of the various suggestions in the Food theme.

Additional material which will be helpful in a cross section of the suggestions contained within this theme are as follows:

STORIES TO BE READ OR TOLD

'A row of carrots' ⎱ From *Stories for all Seasons*
'Using our Talents' ⎰ (National Christian Education Council)

Social Studies

Harvest time should not pass now without some reference to the many children in the world who are hungry. This can apply to any work involving food. The children will know that hunger is a part of the world as this is brought into their homes through programmes on the television. Many agencies will supply material amongst which are Christian Aid, Save the Children, Oxfam.

Religious Education

A responsive psalm for Harvest-time
Psalm 65 (R.V.)
Praise waiteth for Thee, O God.
> *We praise You.*

Thou visitest the earth, and waterest it.
> *We praise You.*

Thou providest corn, when Thou hast prepared the earth.
> *We praise You.*

Thou waterest her furrows, and makest it soft with showers.
> *We praise You.*

The pastures are clothed with flocks; the valleys also are covered over with corn.
> *We praise You.*

They shout for joy; they also sing.
> *We praise You.*

Amen

PRAYERS:

Harvest time prayers can be found in *Praying With Primaries*, by Dorothy R. Wilton (National Christian Education Council), and in Psalm 65, as above. The children can write their own prayers of thanks for food, remembering the people in other lands who work to provide us with the things we need to make us healthy. Prayers can also be written for unfortunate children who are hungry.

HYMNS

Ears of corn are listening } From *New Child Songs*
God made the iron } (Denholm House Press)

> We plough the fields with tractors,
>   With drills we sow the land;
> But growth is still the wondrous gift
>   Of God's almighty hand.
> We add our fertilizers
>   To help the growing grain—
> But for its full fruition
>   It needs God's sun and rain.
> *All good gifts around us. . . .*
>
> With many new machines now
>   We do the work each day;
> We reap the fields with combines,
>   We bale the new-mown hay.
> But it is God who gives us
>   Inventive skills and drives
> Which lighten labour's drudg'ry
>   And give us fuller lives.
> *All good gifts around us. . . .*
> (From Christian Aid, used by permission)

ASSEMBLY

It is quite possible that schools already have their traditions of how the produce brought for the Harvest Festival is to be distributed. However, to link the need of giving to people overseas in addition to people in need at home, perhaps a retiring offering could be made for one of the agencies listed in the Social Studies section, or alternatively the children could be encouraged to bring postage stamps and trading stamps which can then be sent to the organization selected. They can then use the gift to the best advantage.

Further Source Material
FILMSTRIP
Pedro's Chicken (selected frames) (National Christian Education Council)

A LIST OF USEFUL ADDRESSES

Athena Reproductions Ltd., Bishop's Stortford, Herts.
A.V.A. Magazine, 2 Eaton Gate, London SW1 9BL.
Baptist Missionary Society, 93 Gloucester Place, London W.1.
Boosey & Hawkes Ltd., The Hyde, Edgware Road, London NW9 6JN.
British & Foreign Bible Society, 146 Queen Victoria Street, London E.C.4.
Centrehurst Ltd., 72 Brewer Street, London W.1.
Church Information Office, Church House, Dean's Yard, London SW1 3NZ.
Church Missionary Society, 157 Waterloo Road, London S.E.1.
Church Pastoral-Aid Society, Falcon Court, 32 Fleet Street, London E.C.4.
Christian Aid, P.O. Box No. 1, 2 Sloane Gardens, London S.W.1.
Christian Education Movement, International Department, Annandale, North End Road, London NW11 7QX.
Commonwealth Institute, The, Kensington High Street, London W8 6NQ.
Concord Films Council, Nacton, Ipswich, Suffolk.
Concordia Films & Publishing House Ltd., 117-123 Golden Lane, London EC1Y 0TL.

Congregational Council for World Mission, Livingstone House, 11 Cartaret Street, London S.W.1.

Council for Nature, Zoological Gardens, Regent's Park, London N.W.1.

Denholm House Press, Robert Denholm House, Nutfield, Redhill, Surrey RH1 4HW.

Dianna Wyllie Ltd., 3 Park Road, Baker Street, London N.W.1.

Dinosaur Publications Ltd., Beechcroft, Over, Cambridge, CB4 5NE.

E.M.I. Records (The Gramophone Company Ltd.), 142 Wardour Street, London W1V 4AE.

Encyclopaedia Britannica International Ltd., Educational Film Division, Dolcis House, 87-91 New Bond Street, London W1Y 9LA.

Galliard Ltd., Queen Anne's Road, Great Yarmouth, Norfolk.

Geoffrey Chapman Ltd., 18 High Street, Wimbledon, S.W.19.

Guide Dogs for the Blind Association, The, 113 Uxbridge Road, Ealing, London W.5.

Health Education Council, The, Middlesex House, Ealing Road, Wembley, Middlesex, HA0 1HH.

Helen Keller Home, Jerusalem.

High-Fye Music Ltd., 10 Denmark Street, London WC2H 8LU.

Holy Lands Bible Society, High Wycombe, Bucks.

Lutterworth Press, Albion House, Woking, Surrey.

Methodist Missionary Society, 25 Marylebone Road, London N.W.1.

National Christian Education Council, Robert Denholm House, Nutfield, Redhill, Surrey RH1 4HW.

National Gallery, The, Publications Department, Trafalgar Square, London W.C.2.

National Trust, The, 42 Queen Anne's Gate, London SW1H 9DH.

Oxfam, Oxford.

Religious Education Press, Headington Hill Hall, Oxford.

Royal Astronomical Society, The, Burlington House, London W.1.

Royal National Institute for the Blind, The, 224 Great Portland Street, London W1N 6AA.

Royal Society for the Prevention of Cruelty to Animals, The, 105 Jermyn Street, London SW1Y 6EG.

Royal Society for the Protection of Birds, The, The Lodge, Sandy, Bedfordshire.

Save the Children Fund, 29 Queen Anne's Gate, London SW1H 9DH.

School Nature Science Society, 44 Claremont Gardens, Upminster, Essex RM14 1DN.

Slide Centre, The, Portman House, 17 Brodrick Road, London S.W.17.

Society of St. Paul, The, St. Paul's House, Langley, Slough, Bucks.

Souvenir Press Ltd., 95 Mortimer Street, London W1N 8HP.

St. Dunstan's, 191 Marylebone Road, P.O. Box 58, London NW1 5QN.

Tate Gallery, The, Publications Department, Millbank, London S.W.1.

Themescope, P.O. Box No. 5 Cresswell Road, Chesham, Bucks.

Weston Woods Studios Ltd., P.O. Box No. 2, Henley-on-Thames, Oxon.

White Fish Authority, The, 2 Cursitor Street, London E.C.4.

Wildfowl Trust Ltd., The, Slimbridge, Gloucester GL2 7BT.

Wildlife Panda Club, The, Wildlife Youth Service, Marston Court, Manor Road, Wallington, Surrey.

Woodmansterne Ltd., Watford, Herts.